In the Cards,
All That You Were, Are,
or Want to Be

Your mind has an infinite capacity to make connections and to find meanings in disconnected facts or abstract symbols. Gestalt Tarot strips the cards of their traditional meanings, then asks you to find your own meanings in the cards. Thus, Gestalt Tarot allows you to find the symbols, fields of meaning, or patterns that easily represent significant factors in your own life or thought patterns.

In all these ways, Gestalt Tarot is in harmony with the basic tenets of humanistic psychology. It honors human creativity and choices by offering a mutable view of the future, not a glimpse of an unalterable fate. It defines meaning as that which is significant to you, no matter whether it is sense or nonsense to another. And it values the dignity and strength of the individual by empowering you to explore, understand, and guide your own life.

About the Authors

Amber K joined the Temple of the Pagan Way in Chicago, receiving her initiation and ordination there. She has worked with Circle, New Earth Circle, and The Pool of Bast, and helped found the Coven of Our Lady of the Woods (OLW). She has served as Publications Officer and National First Officer of the Covenant of the Goddess, and taught in the Cella (priestess) training program of RCG, a national Dianic network. Her son, Starfire, is a Wiccan security officer.

Azrael Arynn K brings to the Craft her experience as a police officer, race car driver, stockbroker, and architectural designer, as well as a doctorate in law. She is a talented costume designer and ritualist. Both Amber and Azrael are third-degree priestesses in the Ladywood Tradition of Wicca. They met at a Wicca 101 sponsored by Our Lady of the Woods in 1992 and were handfasted in 1994.

The authors have taught many workshops at Pagan festivals and conferences, including Pantheacon, Heartland, UEA, Dragonfest, Florida Samhain Pagan Gathering, Starwood, and others. They are part of the team launching Ardantane, an intertraditional Wiccan seminary to be based near Santa Fe. (For information, write to the Ardantane Project, c/o OLW, P.O. Box 1107, Los Alamos, NM 87544, or see the website at www.Ladywoods.org or www.Ardantane.org.) Amber and Azrael live in Los Alamos, New Mexico. Their home doubles as the OLW covenstead.

To Write to the Authors

If you wish to contact the authors or would like more information about this book, please write to the authors in care of Llewellyn Worldwide and we will forward your request. Both the authors and publisher appreciate hearing from you and learning of your enjoyment of this book and how it has helped you. Llewellyn Worldwide cannot guarantee that every letter written to the authors can be answered, but all will be forwarded. Please write to:

Amber K and Azrael Arynn K
c/o Llewellyn Worldwide
P.O. Box 64383, Dept. 1-56718-008-6
St. Paul, MN 55164-0383, U.S.A.

Please enclose a self-addressed stamped envelope for reply, or $1.00 to cover costs.
If outside U.S.A., enclose international postal reply coupon.

Many of Llewellyn's authors have websites with additional information
and resources. For more information, please visit our website at www.llewellyn.com.

HEART OF TAROT

AN INTUITIVE APPROACH

AMBER K & AZRAEL ARYNN K

2002
Llewellyn Publications
St. Paul, Minnesota, 55164-0383 U.S.A.

FIRST EDITION
First Printing, 2002

Book design and editing by Connie Hill
Cover design by Kevin Brown
Illustrations from *Morgan-Greer* Tarot deck reproduced by permission of U.S. Games Systems, Inc., Stamford, CT 06902 U.S.A. Copyright © 1993 by U.S. Games Systems, Inc. Further reproduction prohibited.

Library of Congress Cataloging-in-Publication Data
K, Amber, 1947–
   Heart of tarot : an intuitive approach / Amber K & Azrael Arynn K — 1st ed.
     p. cm.
   Includes bibliographical references (p.).
   ISBN 1-56718-008-6
     1. Tarot. I. K, Azrael Arynn, 1955– II. Title:

BF1879.T2 K22   2002
133.3'2424 — dc21   2002016074

Llewellyn Worldwide does not participate in, endorse, or have any authority or responsibility concerning private business transactions between our authors and the public.

   All mail addressed to the author is forwarded but the publisher cannot, unless specifically instructed by the author, give out an address or phone number.

   Any Internet references contained in this work are current at publication time, but the publisher cannot guarantee that a specific location will continue to be maintained. Please refer to the publisher's website for links to authors' websites and other sources.

Llewellyn Publications
A Division of Llewellyn Worldwide, Ltd.
P.O. Box 64383, Dept. 1-56718-008-6
St. Paul, MN 55164-0383, U.S.A.
www.llewellyn.com

 Printed in the United States of America on recycled paper

Dedication

For John McClimans:
priest, teacher of teachers, and friend to many.
Merry shall we meet again.

Other Books by Amber K

True Magick (Llewellyn Publications, 1990)

Moonrise: Welcome to Dianic Wicca
(Reformed Congregation of the Goddess, 1992)

Pagan Kids Activity Book (Horned Owl, 1986, 1998)

Covencraft (Llewellyn Publications, 1998)

Preámbulo a la magia (Llewellyn Publications, 1999)

Candlemas: Feast of Flames, with Azrael Arynn K
(Llewellyn Publications, 2001)

Table of Contents

Foreword by M. Macha NightMare   ix

Acknowledgments   xi

Terminology and Grammar   xii

Introduction   xiii

SECTION I: **THE TAROT THROUGH FRESH EYES**

Chapter 1   A Brief History of the Mysterious Tarot   3

Chapter 2   What Is Gestalt Tarot?   11

Chapter 3   The Major Arcana   17

Chapter 4   The Minor Arcana   63

Chapter 5   The Gestalt Tarot Spreads   89

SECTION II: **READING WITH THE GESTALT METHOD**

Chapter 6   Getting Started with Gestalt   105

Chapter 7   Reading for Yourself   111

Chapter 8   The Gestalt Reading   119

Chapter 9   Sample Tarot Readings   141

SECTION III: **THE COMPLEAT TAROT**

Chapter 10   More Spreads   181

Chapter 11   The Professional Reader   205

Chapter 12   Querents Who Present Special Challenges   219

Chapter 13   Teaching the Tarot   229

Chapter 14   Tarot Magick   243

Chapter 15   Summary and Conclusion   259

Appendix I   What Is Gestalt?   261

Appendix II   The Gestalt Reading Step-by-Step   265

Bibliography   Books About Tarot   267

The Circular Nature of Reality

By M. Macha NightMare

Amber K tells of learning this method of reading Tarot from her teachers, Ginny and Dave. Ginny and Dave in turn claim to have learned it from John Patrick McClimans. More than once, dear John told me emphatically that the best magical training he ever had anywhere, of the many places in the United States that he learned magic, was from Ginny and Dave and the Temple of the Pagan Way in Chicago—the very place where Amber learned John's method of reading Tarot.

John read Tarot for lots of people, close friends and total strangers alike. To do this, he shifted his consciousness just enough to disengage the critic and to awaken the intuitive. First, he'd chat a bit about your concerns, then ask you to shuffle the deck while thinking of your query or your situation. While the querent shuffled, John closed his eyes, took a few deep breaths, and opened his eyes with them just a bit unfocused.

John read for me many times. He read at his house, in restaurants, at fairs, in my home, at friends' homes. He was a unique and magical man, twinkling of eye, shiny of head, fuzzy of face, portly of belly. As stout as he was, he had delicate features and a peculiar and unlikely elfin quality.

For about three years, John and I and four other women met one Sunday a month for a Tarot potluck. It was just like John, gynophiliac that he was, to be the only male among a sisterhood.

In 1996 John passed through the veil into the world of spirit. When Amber and I talked of John's death, we discovered two things: she found out that John and I were close, and that John inspired in her the notion of Gestalt Tarot. Amber told me John had encouraged her to write about it. That was John, shining his adoring eyes on his friends, especially women, and seeing the best in them. So I followed John's recommendation by challenging Amber to fulfill that dream, and offering to write a foreword if she wrote the book. That challenge has now been met.

John Patrick McClimans was my counsel and confidante, who sometimes used Tarot to give me guidance, and we all miss him terribly. Now John is our ancestor, yet his work lives in Amber's book. She does John honor.

M. Macha NightMare

෨

Acknowledgments

No book is written in a vacuum. We want to thank the following people who made this work possible or at least helped immensely:

- John McClimans, who first developed Gestalt Tarot into a useful system and shared it

- Amber's first teachers in the Craft, Ginny and Dave, who passed it along to her

- The wonderful folks at Llewellyn, most especially Nancy Mostad and Barbara Wright

- The folks at U.S. Games Systems, who hold the copyright on the *Morgan-Greer* deck and gave us permission to use it in the sample spreads here

- Our covenmates who reviewed the draft and made many excellent suggestions: Tehom, for her editorial suggestions; Cedar, Joan of the Bow, and Merlyn

- All the folks who have read Tarot for us, and have let us read for them, and allowed us to teach them what we know of the Tarot; from the students, the teacher learns

Thank you all.

Terminology and Grammar

We do not believe in the "generic masculine" (the sexist notion that "he" refers to people of both sexes) and have tried to avoid it. Unfortunately, it is awkward to include both genders in every sentence, such as "He or she is fortunate if he or she can find a Tarot reader to his or her liking." Instead, we have often used "they" and "their" to indicate the indeterminate singular as well as the plural. For example, "If a Tarot reader wants to be their best, they had better be prepared to work hard." We know perfectly well that this is ungrammatical by conservative standards, but it is becoming increasingly commonplace in actual usage—and it's not sexist.

Introduction

This is the story of a remarkable method of reading the Tarot cards, created by a remarkable man—John McClimans. We hope you will find, as we have, that this system brings a clarity and power to the cards that have eluded all too many would-be readers.

In Gestalt Tarot, the reader's job is to ask questions, listen carefully, and lead the seeker or client in simple exercises that help them discover their own answers. The reader is a guide or facilitator, rather than a psychic or advisor. He or she does not memorize official meanings for each card and repeat them to the seeker; each card means whatever the seeker thinks it does. Because the insights of the reading are discovered and owned by the seeker, they are highly personal, immediately relevant, and very empowering.

Amber first learned Gestalt Tarot during her studies at the Temple of the Pagan Way in Chicago. Her teachers, who declined the temptation to adopt impressive titles and secret Craft names, were called Dave and Ginny. They freely shared their knowledge and skills; and this particular skill they credited to the creative mind of one of their teachers, John McClimans.

Amber fell in love with Gestalt Tarot. She had never felt comfortable with the stiff, wooden recital of card meanings memorized from a book ("You will meet a tall authoritative man [with a sword and scepter?] who will bring you a message . . ."). Nor did she like relying on her psychic skills for the interpretations ("I sense victory in your future, I think, or someone's future anyway, at least it feels like victory . . ."). Here is a method that draws its truths from the querent's own mind, and empowers the querent in doing so.

Enthusiastically she began spreading the word, teaching her own students the method as she understood it. But as she taught she was conscious of a certain uneasiness about the accuracy and purity of what she was transmitting. The technique was passed from John to Ginny and Dave to Amber pretty much by word of mouth, and she had no way to know if she was unintentionally straying from the original system.

John McClimans had moved to California before Amber had a chance to meet him. Several years after she had learned Gestalt Tarot, they finally connected. Amber thanked him profusely for inventing the system and suggested that he write it down and publish a book, so it wouldn't be lost or corrupted. His reply startled her a bit: "Well, suppose you write it?" Since he didn't want to, Amber decided to consider that option and promptly put it on the back burner with a bevy of other book ideas.

A few years after that conversation, John was no longer with us. Now we feel a certain obligation to honor his memory and preserve a fascinating technique by sharing this book with the world—or at least those Tarot aficionados who will appreciate it. We hope we have recorded the technique with a depth and accuracy John would have approved.

What will you find in this book? First, a little of the history of Tarot in general, insofar as it is known or guessed. Then we will begin exploring the Gestalt system of reading, and alternative ways in which the cards can be interpreted. Both a full Gestalt spread (the pattern in which the cards are laid out) and a short version are shown. A step-by-step reading method is provided, and two sample readings to give you a feel for how the technique works in practice. Then a selection of different spreads are shown that can be used with the Gestalt method or any other.

Following this, we will offer some practical suggestions for anyone who may wish to read professionally, including a look at some of the more challenging kinds of clients you may encounter.

The next section provides some helpful tools for those who teach Tarot. You may not be teaching now, but may be asked to lead a class someday, once you have gained some experience. The final major chapter explains ways that you can use Tarot cards in magick for healing, personal growth, and other positive goals.

Gestalt Tarot is a powerful tool for those who value deep knowledge, self-understanding, and personal growth. It is a window into our subjective present and potential futures. On behalf of John McClimans and those who have shared it throughout the Tarot world, we offer you this gift.

Blessed be,
Amber K and Azrael Arynn K
Los Alamos, New Mexico
January, 2001

Section 1

❧ | ☙

The Tarot Through Fresh Eyes

Chapter 1

A Brief History of the Mysterious Tarot

Who created the first Tarot deck? When did it happen? What purpose did they have in mind for the cards?

Was it a lonely monk snowbound in the Italian Alps? Was it a priestess of the lost continent of Atlantis, seeking to preserve the spiritual teachings of the island empire? Was it a merchant from the Italian city-states, who followed the Silk Road to China, bringing home chests of rare spices—and the idea for Tarot?

The true origin of the Tarot cards is lost in the mists of time, although there are plenty of colorful (and unprovable) theories. No one even knows for certain what the name means.

Terminology

Webster's Unabridged Encyclopedic Dictionary defines Tarot as "any of a set of twenty-two playing cards bearing allegorical representations, used for fortunetelling and as trump cards in tarock," a card game dating from the Renaissance and still popular in central Europe.

In fifteenth-century Italy, the twenty-two Major Arcana were called *trionfi*, or in the Latin *triumphi*, now trumps. By the sixteenth century the trionfi were added to the card game tarocchi, to create the seventy-eight-card Tarot deck common today. Tarot is the French derivative of *tarocchi*.

The original meaning of Tarot or tarocchi is uncertain, although a popular theory says that it is from the Egyptian *tar* (road) and *ro* (royal or king's), therefore meaning "the royal road."

Today the trumps are often called the Major Arcana (arcana means secrets or mysteries) and the other cards are referred to as the Minor Arcana.

The Major Arcana

Stuart Kaplan, in his *Encyclopedia of Tarot*, (Stamford Conn., U.S. Games Systems, 1978, 1985, 1990) says that the "Major Arcana cards depict . . . the continuous and ever-changing physical and spiritual forces affecting humanity. To some persons, the trump cards are a pictorial processional of life's fateful events."

The earliest known list of trumps comes from a Christian priest's treatise against gambling in the fifteenth century. This particular clergyman reviled the Tarot as mocking the Church because it included cards such as the Popess; in his same generation, other men in holy orders extolled the virtues of the cards as providing a morally instructive model of the way society was supposed to be structured. As translated from Latin, the trumps were:

1. The Magician, or Juggler.
2. The Empress.
3. The Emperor.
4. The Popess (now High Priestess).
5. The Pope (now Hierophant).
6. Temperance.
7. The Lovers, or Love.
8. The Chariot.
9. Strength.
10. The Wheel, or Wheel of Fortune.
11. The Hermit, or Father Time.
12. The Hanged Man.
13. Death.
14. The Devil.
15. The Arrow (now The Tower).

16. The Star.

17. The Moon.

18. The Sun.

19. The Angel (now Judgment).

20. Justice.

21. The World.

22. The Fool.

Over the centuries many scholars have tried to discover links or correspondences between the Tarot cards and other symbolic systems: the characters of the alphabet, the signs of the zodiac, the planets, the elements, the sephiroth of the Qabalah, the paths from one sephira to another, and so on. The human mind is capable of creating hugely elaborate and complicated systems, and they bear as much or as little relation to reality (whatever that may be) as you choose to believe.

The Minor Arcana

The cards of the Minor Arcana (fifty-six of them in the more standard decks) are divided into four suits, probably the origins of the four suits in modern decks of playing cards. These are:

- Swords (corresponding to Spades)

- Wands (sometimes called rods, staves, batons, or scepters, corresponding to Clubs)

- Cups (corresponding to Hearts)

- Pentacles (sometimes called coins, corresponding to Diamonds)

As with the Major Arcana, people love to add all kinds of symbolic correspondences to the suits; they may represent the four Elements, the four cardinal virtues, the four classes of society, and so on. For example, some of the symbolic links look like those on the following page.

Swords =	Air =	Justice =	Knights and nobles
Wands =	Fire =	Fortitude =	Peasants
Cups =	Water =	Faith =	Clergy
Pentacles =	Earth =	Charity =	Merchants

The Minor Arcana are further divided into the court cards and the pip cards. The court cards include Kings, Queens, Knights, and Pages in most decks. In many of the early decks, these were portrayed as historical and mythological figures, such as famous kings and warriors.

The remaining cards are called pip cards because in the first decks, they did not have pictures or scenes but only swords, wands, cups, or pentacles in the appropriate numbers. For example, the Three of Cups originally had only three stylized cups depicted on it. In the popular *Rider-Waite* deck used today, the Three of Cups shows a scene with three maidens dancing together in a garden, each lifting a chalice in a toast or salute.

It appears that the Major and Minor Arcana originated as separate systems, and were later joined. The Major Arcana were probably allegorical or instructional in the beginning, while the Minor Arcana may have been simply a card game. The Minor Arcana have a split lineage, surviving today both in common playing cards and in a more exalted form in the Tarot.

The Origins of the Tarot

No one knows exactly where or when the Tarot was invented, nor the purpose. Theories abound; Stuart Kaplan lists seventy-eight possible origins in *The Encyclopedia of Tarot*. Here are but a few.

The Atlantis Theory

When the great sea empire was overwhelmed and sank beneath the waves, a handful of priests and teachers survived and made their way to other lands, there to preserve what they could of Atlantean culture. These lonely colonies became the seeds of the Minoan, Egyptian, and Mayan civilizations. To make sure that their most important spiritual teachings would survive, the survivors encapsulated the essence in the Tarot.

The Egyptian Theory

The Book of Thoth, named after the ibis-headed god of literature and wisdom, held a "synthesis of all human knowledge and profound mysticism." (Kaplan) The Tarot could be the unbound pages of this sacred book. It may actually have been written by the legendary magician Hermes Trismegistus, and preserved in a secret chamber, under the Sphinx or in the Great Pyramid, where the twenty-two images of the Major Arcana are carved. Or it could be another version of the Tablet Isiaca, a cryptic stone tablet (possibly an altar top dedicated to Isis) that disappeared centuries ago.

Alternatively, when the Library at Alexandria was destroyed, learned men gathered at Fez and developed the Tarot as a pictorial language to communicate with each other and preserve universal spiritual truths and esoteric teachings (sound familiar?). The Gypsies (from a slang term for "Egyptians," though the Romany peoples probably actually originated in India) carried the Tarot with them on their wanderings and spread it throughout Europe.

The Indian Theory

The four suits represented the four classes of Hindu society: the Cups stood for the Brahmins or priestly class, the Swords for Kshatriyas who were the nobility and warriors, the Coins for Vaisya or merchants and artisans, and the Wands for Sudras or farmers. There are also potential links to Buddhism: the Fool may symbolize a wandering monk on his path to enlightenment.

The Jewish Theory

There are twenty-two Major Arcana, twenty-two letters in the Hebrew Alphabet, and twenty-two paths on the Tree of Life from the Qabalah. There are four suits in the Tarot, and four letters in the name of God: JHVH. There are ten pips in the Minor Arcana (Ace through Ten), and ten spheres or sephiroth on the Tree. Coincidence? Some think not.

The Chinese Theory

Nothing in the Tarot looks Chinese, but playing cards were in use in China before the eleventh century, so perhaps the idea was brought back by Marco Polo or someone else, and instantly Europeanized.

The Gnostic Theory

Gnosticism was a combination of Indian, Chaldean, Persian, and Egyptian magic, with Greek philosophy, Qabalah, and early Christian teachings thrown in, and a dollop of Pagan influence. Gnostics thought that one could escape from this world by possessing esoteric knowledge. The Roman Catholic Church thought this was totally heretical. The Tarot looks like the sort of thing the Gnostics would dream up; they loved to look mysterious, rather than just reveal Universal Truths straight out and be done with it.

The Saracen Theory

Possibly the Crusaders brought back Tarot decks as souvenirs from the land of the Saracens. This would explain why the cards were condemned by Church fathers as heretical, the "Devil's picture book." If it came from the "Infidels" it couldn't be respectable. (Note that the Saracens had the last laugh: guess where the concept of zero in math came from?)

The Knights Templar Theory

In the fourteenth century, the Knights Templar may have decided to preserve their understanding of the Grail legends and mysteries by creating the Tarot. The four "Grail Hallows" or Christian sacred objects were symbolized by the suits: the Sword is King David's "sword of the spirit"; the Cup is the Grail used at the Last Supper; the Pentacle is the plate that held the bread; and the Wand is the lance of Longinus, the spear used to pierce Jesus' side at the crucifixion.

The Celtic Pagan Theory

The suits could represent the Four Treasures of Ireland and the Tuatha de Danaan: the Sword is the invincible Sword of Nuada, god of the sea and wealth; the Cup is the Cauldron called "Undry," always magically filled with food, belonging to Dagda, the "Good God" or "All-Father"; the Pentacle is the Stone of Fal, the coronation seat of Ireland, sometimes called the Siege Perilous; and the Wand is the Spear of Lugh, god of the sun, warrior hero, skilled in all crafts.

The Facts So Far

In 1377, Brother Johannes of Bredfeld in Switzerland described a game of cards that outlined society's structure. As with the Indian theory, Cups represented churchmen, Swords symbolized the aristocracy, Coins were merchants, and Wands or Clubs stood for the peasantry. There was a moral lesson in all this: know your place.

Most of the early trumps were from northern Italy, and created in the late 1300s. In France their first documented appearance was in 1392, under Charles VI. Seventeen cards from this "Gringonneur" deck still exist.

So it would appear that the first trumps were probably created in Italy in the mid to late fourteenth century, probably by a monk who worked in a scriptorium and therefore had both artistic skills and access to pens and paint.

The Uses of Tarot

Fortunetelling. The old woman in a shawl and gold hoop earrings, cackling over worn and faded cards by lamplight: "I see love in your future, a tall and handsome gentleman. . . ." Is this what Tarot is all about?

Well, in a sense. Some readers actually do predictive readings for others. The shawl and the hoop earrings may have been replaced by a T-shirt and jeans, but that reading method hasn't changed much in the six centuries Tarot has been around.

Tarot can also be a tool for gaining self-insight and understanding of the trends in one's life—which is what Gestalt Tarot is all about. It can easily be used as a counseling tool.

For those who practice magick—the real stuff, not stage illusions—Tarot cards can help to banish negativity, achieve goals, catalyze personal change, or even work spells for healing, safe travel, or meeting that special someone. Some of these magickal uses are discussed in a later chapter.

The beauty of the different designs makes Tarot cards an enjoyable collectible for art lovers; and because the cards are a window into society in earlier times, they will intrigue anyone with an interest in history.

On the lighter side, Tarot can be fun. Related card games such as tarock exist for recreation and amusement. Though these games are not within the scope of this book, information on them is available in libraries or on the Internet.

Tarot Decks Today

Early Tarot decks were commissioned by noblemen, individually hand-painted and sometimes gilded. Each was a unique work of art.

Today Tarot decks are printed by the millions by a handful of companies, and many new decks have been designed. Dozens of designs are easily available, and dozens more are out of print and therefore have become collectors' items. We will discuss some of the more well-known and easily available decks in chapter 6. For an amazingly extensive list of decks with illustrations, including the most ancient decks known, see Stuart Kaplan's *Encyclopedia of Tarot*.

We are experiencing a renaissance and creative flowering of Tarot unlike any-thing seen in centuries; perhaps this is part of a tide in history, that ebbs and flows between myth and reason. For millennia, human affairs were guided by faith, superstition, and passion; the tide began to change with the Reformation, the "Age of Enlightenment," and the advent of the scientific method. In the wake of tremendous strides in technology and secular understanding came a popular cul-ture that leaned toward the mechanical and technical; art and religion waned, the Dreamtime ended.

Yet now we find a resurgence of spirituality in many forms, almost in tandem with the technological revolution. In this New Age, it is not uncommon to find people surfing the Internet and upgrading their software in the morning, and meditating or doing artwork the same afternoon. Perhaps we are seeing the leading edge of a great rebalancing in Western civilization, where the intuitive, imaginative, dreaming side of the human mind is again valued as much as the logical and scientific part. If so, Tarot is part of it all.

A Brief

History

of the

Mysterious

Tarot

Chapter 2

What Is Gestalt Tarot?

Tarot reading is often a solitary process performed by an individual for personal guidance or enlightenment. However, it can also involve two people, a *querent* and a *reader*. The querent is the person seeking information or guidance, and the reader provides that guidance or facilitates the process for the querent.

There are three major ways to read the Tarot. First, the reader may memorize and repeat the card meanings listed in a book, often one written by the creator of that particular deck design. Second, the reader may psychically interpret the cards. (Some readers may combine these methods, using the official card meanings as a foundation, and adding their own insights into the process.) And third, the querent may search within for the meanings of the cards, with assistance from the reader. This third way is called Gestalt Tarot.

Any of these methods may produce an insightful and satisfying reading, depending on the knowledge and skill of the reader. We believe that Gestalt readings have special advantages in many situations.

The Memorization Method

The first method, working from a deck designer's list of card meanings, rests on two assumptions for its efficacy. First, we hope that the designer and author of any given deck have a profound understanding of human nature, and that they can express each aspect of it in a few luminous paragraphs, and that these truths are expressed in a manner that any querent can understand and apply to their own life. This is a challenge for any communicator. When two people collaborate on a deck—an artist and a writer—we must hope that they perfectly understand each other, and that the writer is explaining exactly what the artist meant or vice versa.

Where one person designs, draws, and describes the entire deck, we must hope for a Da Vinci: philosopher, artist, and writer in one package. Otherwise we might find a deck based on profound insights, but badly drawn; or a beautiful deck that is shallow conceptually; or a deep and lovely deck that is explained in banal or confusing terms. In fact, all these sorts of decks are on the market, as well as some that really do work well on all levels.

The second assumption about the memorization method presents more difficulty. We have to assume that some force or agency has caused the reader to deal, or the querent to select, exactly those cards that apply to their particular life situation. Because if the cards have fixed meanings, but turn up randomly, then the querent may as well buy a "magic 8-ball" in a novelty store or flip a coin for guidance.

Is there an agency mysteriously choosing the right cards for the occasion? A guardian angel? A spirit guide? The "Spirit of the Tarot?" A deity? Perhaps.

Many people would like to believe that benevolent spirits are watching from the astral planes, willing to advise us on our love lives or personal problems. This may or may not be true, but even if it is, there is great potential for misunderstanding when one communicates with the spirit world at all. You cannot always be positive that you have connected with the spirit you want to talk to, or that the spirit is entirely knowledgeable on the question, or even being honest with you. When the Tarot is factored in to the communication, the sometimes ambiguous or multiple meanings of the cards add another layer of potential error.

Psychic Tarot

The second option is to trust the psychic powers of the reader. Some readers may be able to intuitively choose the cards with appropriate book meanings for the querent's situation. Others say that the cards have no fixed meanings, but they can psychically discover what meaning a particular card has for that particular client.

Now clearly, some individuals are more intuitive, insightful, and sensitive to subtle cues than others. Doubtless these qualities can be intentionally developed (to a degree) by anyone, just as most people can learn to hit a baseball or pick out "Chopsticks" on a piano, but not everyone can be the Babe Ruth or Beethoven of psychic Tarot readers.

Use of the psychic method places an enormous responsibility on the reader. Querents who ask for a Tarot reading are obviously predisposed to believe what is told them, and many will make important life decisions based on the reading. How many of us trust our psychic accuracy enough to want other people to guide their lives by it? What if we are not as insightful as we would like to think, or are simply having an off day, and we tell the querent something that leads to disaster? For those of us who are not highly skilled psychics, the psychic method has risks to the welfare of others (and our own consciences) that we might not care to take.

Tarot as a Tool of Empowerment

We might ask ourselves, where does the insight and understanding come from in each method? Who is the arbiter of meaning, the authority? In the first case, the information comes ultimately from the designer of the deck who prescribed those particular cards' meanings. The reader, having memorized the official meanings, becomes the purveyor of the Word. There may be no ego involvement happening, but like it or not, the fact is inescapable: the reader has the cards' meanings and the querent doesn't. The querent, whose questions are at issue, sits passively and tries to see some relevance in what they are being told.

In the second case, the reader spurns the printed doctrine and relies on their psychic abilities to divine what a particular card means for this particular querent at this time. Presumably the reader has, or believes they have, a special talent for understanding the querent's life better than the querent can. The reading may be accurate, insightful, and tremendously helpful in certain ways; but once again, the insight and authority rest firmly in the hands of the reader, and the querent listens passively as a friend, acquaintance, or total stranger explains their life to them.

In the third case, Gestalt Tarot, the reader's job is to ask *open-ended* questions, engage in reflective listening, and suggest experiences that help the querent follow a thread of meaning, until the querent finds an insight that makes perfect sense to that individual. The reader is a neutral guide, neither sage nor psychic, who is there to facilitate the quest. The querent finds their own answers and is strengthened as a result. The answers are the querent's answers, discovered and owned by them. The authority and responsibility for the insights, as for all of their life, rest squarely where they belong—in the hands of the querent.

We might wonder whether *all* querents really want that kind of responsibility. The answer is "no." After all, it is easier (and more entertaining) to have someone else explain us to ourselves, than it is to grub around in our subconscious minds and find the truth for ourselves—just as it is easier to watch football on television than it is to run out on the field and endure the sweaty, muscular reality of the game firsthand. Just as it is far easier to blame or credit Fate, the gods, or a Tarot reader for what happens to us than it is to accept responsibility for our own lives.

Some querents will come to us expecting to find an Authority cloaked in a mantle of arcane knowledge and spiritual superiority. When they do not find what they expect, they may be confused even suspicious, thinking: "You must know what's happening in my life; why won't you just tell me so I can pay you and go home?"

Where does that leave us as Tarot readers? We need not buy into a client's voluntary impotence. Just because lots of people are willing to hand over their power, their responsibility, and their choices does not mean that we have to accept them. We can say, "You may choose to surrender your responsibility for understanding and directing your life, but I will not fill the void. I am not your parent, nor your religious guru. Most importantly, I am not you, and I will not accept control or guidance of any part of your life."

And let us not forget that there are people willing and eager to seek their own meaning, accept spiritual and moral responsibility for their actions, and choose their own paths. For these we can be allies and friends; they will value our skills while not thrusting their independence into our unwilling hands.

Gestalt Psychology and Tarot

Gestalt psychology had its beginnings early in the twentieth century, when German psychologists noticed that the human brain, presented with some sensory information (such as a series of pictures flickering past), has the ability to create a whole, a unity, or a "gestalt" from the pieces.

Since then, gestalt psychology has grown to emphasize that human beings can best be understood as whole beings—mental, emotional, physical, and even spiritual—rather than as complicated collections of parts. When something bad happens to a person, the wound cannot always be fixed by healing (or replacing) only the obviously faulty bit, because every part of us is interconnected and every part affects the whole. So, for example, an emotionally distraught person will think differently than usual, and also be more vulnerable to illness.

To take gestalt a step farther, individuals can be understood only as part of their whole environment. None of us exists free-floating, immutable and untouchable by what is around us. We express different personas in the differing spheres we inhabit: at the workplace, in the family home, out with friends, grocery shopping. We occcupy many roles, and the insights that illuminate one role in one environment may not be useful elsewhere.

Gestalt Tarot attempts to elicit several facets of a whole person, or explore an issue in the context of a person's whole life. Because the querent provides the raw information, and usually the interpretation of it, the picture that emerges is more immediate, more relevant, more *real*, than a second-hand reading can be.

But is not the querent's view more subjective than that of a reader? Is it not vulnerable to wishful thinking, prejudices, and selective blindness? It can be, but the Tarot has the great virtue of allowing querents to see themselves one step removed: first as the Fool, the Emperor, or the Hanged Man, and only then as themselves. Querents can look at the archetypal images of the Tarot more clearly than they can see into their own hearts; only later do they realize that their hearts have been projected onto the canvas of the cards, and that they have been looking at themselves the whole time.

Besides, the reader is certainly just as subjective as any querent. We all perceive the world through our own filters. If we are to choose between the subjective viewpoint of the querent or the reader, at least the querent's view is much more relevant to the task at hand. After all, the reading is about the querent.

This may seem like a passive way to help the querent understand their life; it is very different from, say, a therapist who dazzles a client with a brilliant analysis of their underlying issues from a traumatic childhood. However, it is a lot more useful than any brilliant insight you could provide—because it comes from the querent. The querent's insight into their own life is immeasurably more valid, more useful, more *real*—because of the source. My insight into my life is going to stick with me and get used. I own it. I might embrace it and use it to change my life. Your insight into my life might be accurate, but it's going to have no more emotional impact than the "Dear Abby" column I read in the newspaper last week.

In a sense, what we are doing with Gestalt Tarot is giving querents time and tools to think about their lives and come to understand themselves a little better. Thinking about our lives is almost a luxury for some of us; our hectic, fast-paced schedules don't allow much space for reflection. When we do find a free moment, there are a thousand things demanding our attention: family, coworkers, churches and clubs, advertisements, television, radio. It is often easier to give in, to give away all our time and thoughts to the myriad voices around us, than to shut them out for an hour, breathe, and think.

Occasionally we may find that inward time. A visit to a therapist's office. A walk in the woods. A heart-to-heart talk with a new love, or a get-away retreat with the beloved we have been with for years. A Gestalt Tarot reading may be one of the few opportunities for an individual to consider the big questions: "Who am I? Why am I here? Where am I going, and where do I want to go?"

Humanistic psychology reminds us that we live in relationship; that when our relationships with other people and the rest of our environment are healthy, we live in a state of mental and emotional health—a state of grace, in the most immanent, down-to-earth, right-here, right-now sense. When we are out of harmony with our environment (physical, biological, social—in any sense), we manifest that imbalance or antagonism. In either case, the relationships appear in the cards of a Gestalt Tarot spread.

In a way Gestalt Tarot is like a Rorschach test. The Rorschach is a psychological tool in which people are shown abstract, free-form shapes and asked to tell what they see. Originally the shapes were actually inkblots, made by pouring a little ink on a paper and folding it once, so the resulting shape would be symmetrical. One person might look at a given blot and see a wolf's head, and another might see a butterfly. Psychologists can tell a lot about an individual's personality based on what he or she imagines the blots to look like.

Another psychological tool that comes even closer to Gestalt Tarot is the Thematic Apperception Test, or TAT, in which a client is shown a picture of people engaged in various activities, and asked to make up a story that explains the picture. The client will usually create a story that illuminates their own attitudes, emotions, and life issues.

In the same way, what we have known in our personal histories we see in the cards. What we experience as our present reality, we see in the cards. What we desire for the future, we see in the cards. All that we were, are, or want to be is there.

The human mind has an infinite capacity to make connections and to find meaning in disconnected facts or abstract symbols. Gestalt Tarot strips the cards of their traditional meanings, then asks the querent to find their own meanings in the cards. Thus, Gestalt Tarot allows the querent to find the symbols, fields of meaning, sets, or patterns that easily represent significant factors in the querent's own life or thought patterns.

In all these ways, Gestalt Tarot is in harmony with the basic tenets of humanistic psychology. It focuses on the querent's experiences and perceptions, not those of the reader. It honors human creativity and choices by offering a mutable view of the future, not a glimpse of unalterable fate. It defines meaning as that which is significant to the querent, no matter whether it is sense or nonsense to another. And it values the dignity and strength of the individual by empowering the querent to explore, understand, and guide their own life.

Chapter 3

The Major
Arcana

The Major Arcana or "greater mysteries" have always been the heart of Tarot. As mentioned in chapter 1, some believe that the Minor Arcana were another system entirely, grafted on to Tarot for reasons unknown.

In the earliest decks still surviving, the Major Arcana are usually illustrated with a single figure, or at most two or three. The Minor Arcana have no human figures; the Three of Cups depicts three cups, and so on. This makes them fairly useless for Gestalt purposes, but fortunately more recent decks are more imaginative; they depict interesting scenes, often with two or more figures interacting. Every card is like a snapshot from a story, and there are as many stories in a single card as there are people to tell them.

At this point, a traditional Tarot book would explain the official meaning of each Major Arcanum. Rather than that, to give an idea of the range of possible meanings, we will look at each card from at least four perspectives. One is a synopsis of traditional meanings for that card, and three are interpretations that might occur during Gestalt readings, as expressed by imaginary querents. The actual range of possible meanings is, of course, practically infinite. We will use the *Morgan-Greer* deck, which is our favorite and an excellent deck for Gestalt Tarot.

The Fool

Some traditional meanings: Everyman on his spiritual journey through life; extravagance, folly, and bewrayment (betrayal); the innocent unaware of hazard, protected by God; a vital choice ahead.

One alternate meaning: "He?, she?, is walking into danger; his animal ally (power animal, totem animal, younger-self animal) is trying to warn him but he hasn't been listening."

Another: "That's me . . . I think I'm searching for something, maybe going on a vision quest."

Another: "It looks like someone on their way to a celebration or festival; she's wearing bright clothing, with a wreath and feather in her hair, bringing food and flowers to the gathering."

What does this card mean to you? Write your notes in the space below:

_____

_____

_____

_____

_____

_____

_____

_____

_____

_____

_____

_____

_____

_____

0 — THE FOOL

The Magician

Some traditional meanings: Skill, self-confidence, will; occult wisdom; the ability to transform one's life, or to take power and manifest change.

One alternate meaning: "It feels very closed in; there's this huge wall behind the magician. But I think he's chosen to be there. He's hidden himself away in this little walled garden where he can feel in control of his life."

Another: "The first thing I notice is his eyes. Either they're closed or he's blind. But he's lifting this thing, I think it's a scroll . . . it's like he can't see anything for himself anymore, he just believes whatever's written on the scroll."

Another: "This guy is very challenging, or demanding. I mean, he's offering you two choices: 'up or down, my way or the highway'. He's demanding an answer."

What does this card mean to you? Write your notes in the space below:

I — THE MAGICIAN

The High Priestess

Some traditional meanings: Mystery, wisdom, hidden influences, the future unrevealed; creative forces of the subconscious; the querent's higher nature or spiritual understanding; a woman of great intuition and inner illumination.

One alternate meaning: "The priestess has this secret information about magick and the mysteries of life. She's the guardian, it's in the scrolls in her lap or maybe behind the drapery. She's waiting to see if I'm worthy to know."

Another: "I think she's asleep. The moon under her feet means she's dreaming. She's so calm, so serene, nothing can shake her."

Another: "This woman is very covered, wearing lots of skirts and capes and veils. She's protecting herself, or trying to . . . with her knowledge, her wisdom. But I don't think it will work."

What does this card mean to you? Write your notes in the space below:

The Empress

Some traditional meanings: Marriage; fruitfulness, wealth, and abundance; power and capability in the material world; fertility for parents, farmers, or artists.

One alternate meaning: "I would say that she's a very giving person—maybe it's the heart here on her bodice. She has a shield, she has a flower, she wants to protect everyone and make them happy."

Another: "I keep looking at that tiny little pumpkin by her foot. She probably doesn't even know it's there, and she could step on it and squish it by accident. But if someone took care of it, it could grow up and become a splendid, big pumpkin."

Another: "I worry about all that water behind her. This waterfall is pouring down and the water's rising; soon it's going to reach her, and she doesn't even realize."

What does this card mean to you? Write your notes in the space below:

III — THE EMPRESS

The Emperor

Some traditional meanings: Stability, temporal power, protection; reason and conviction, intelligence dominant over passion; authority, will, government and leadership.

One alternate meaning: "I think he's very sad. He's got all this power, but he's alone. I think he wishes he were just a regular person so he could enjoy his family and simple pleasures."

Another: "He reminds me of my grandfather, which is odd, because grand-dad wasn't powerful or rich. But he was very calm and strong, like this person; and usually pretty relaxed . . . look, this king has his legs crossed like, ho-hum, another day running the world."

Another: "He's got a sword, but he's not holding it as though he's about to use it. His scepter is in his right hand; he'll use his authority, and back it up with force only if he has to."

What does this card mean to you? Write your notes in the space below:

IV — THE EMPEROR

The Hierophant

(Also called the Pope)

Some traditional meanings: Religion institutionalized, religious authority, the outer forms and trappings; hierarchy and servitude; rigidity and bureaucracy; the need for conformity and social approval.

One alternate meaning: "This is some mighty person who's giving his blessing or gifts, like land and wealth. I don't think you could get very far if this guy didn't like you."

Another: "This staff reminds me of a telephone pole. Communications. Like he's a messenger, coming to bring important news. The keys could be part of that. Some message that will unlock my whole future."

Another: "His eyes look red to me. That's creepy. Like he's officially some important church leader, but he's been possessed by the devil or taken over by aliens."

What does this card mean to you? Write your notes in the space below:

_____

_____

_____

_____

_____

_____

_____

_____

_____

_____

_____

29

The

Major

Arcana

The Lovers

Some traditional meanings: Attraction, love, and beauty; finding one's soulmate; harmony between the inner self and outer life; the power of choice; the "struggle between sacred and profane love."

One alternate meaning: "He wants to make love but she's reluctant; she's hesitating for some reason. There's an invisible wall between them. Maybe she doesn't quite trust him."

Another: "This is pure lust to me. This wild man comes out of the woods and finds this lady sunbathing in the garden, and they both go crazy sexually."

Another: "Well, they're both naked and it's the Lovers, but there's something else going on here. They're really looking at each other, really trying to communicate, to get past the man-woman thing and connect on some other level besides the physical."

What does this card mean to you? Write your notes in the space below:

_____

_____

_____

_____

_____

_____

_____

_____

_____

_____

_____

_____

_____

The Chariot

Some traditional meanings: Triumph in conflict or over difficulties of all kinds; conquest and greatness; rescue or succor; mastery over one's dual nature or animal passions.

One alternate meaning: "This guy is about to run me down. Whoa, reckless driver here. Get out of the way or you're dead meat."

Another: "The horses look like they're headed in different directions. There's a tremendous amount of energy here, but it doesn't know which way to go. The charioteer had better decide soon or his chariot's going to get torn in half."

Another: "The chariot driver reminds me of King Arthur. I'm remembering 'the once and future king,' like this is Arthur returning from Avalon in Britain's hour of peril. Sometimes when you've just about given up on someone, they come through for you. Which is confusing, then you don't know where you stand."

What does this card mean to you? Write your notes in the space below:

33

The

Major

Arcana

Strength

(Also called Force or Fortitude)

Some traditional meanings: Power, courage, success; love overcoming hate; spiritual nature overcoming carnal desires, animal nature, or material powers.

One alternate meaning: "The lion was dead, and she's bringing it back to life. She's a healer. Or maybe She's the Goddess, who brings life to all things."

Another: "The woman is trying to get the lion to close its mouth. I think it was roaring and frightening everyone and making a huge disruption, and she's teaching it about humility and when to be silent."

Another: "She's treating this big lion like a little pussycat, trying to cuddle it and pet it. The lion doesn't like that, and I think she's about to get bitten big time."

What does this card mean to you? Write your notes in the space below:

VIII — STRENGTH

The Hermit

Some traditional meanings: Prudence and caution; treason or trickery; wisdom from above; a solitary spiritual quest, or finding a guide.

One alternate meaning: "There's a star in the lantern. This old man has climbed to the top of a mountain and captured a star out of the sky. Of course, everyone thought he was crazy, but he did it. He proved that anything is possible—never give up your dreams, no matter how impossible they seem."

Another: "Maybe the light in the lantern represents his accumulated knowledge and wisdom. It's been with him all his life, growing brighter and clearer, and now he's come out here to set it free. He's been a scholar or mystic all his life, and now he's decided to teach and share his knowledge with the world."

Another: "He's holding up a beacon of light in this harsh winter landscape, in case there are any travelers lost out there in the snow. Only twice in his life has anyone seen the light and found him, and one of those wasn't really lost. But once he saved a life, and now every night he goes out, just in case."

What does this card mean to you? Write your notes in the space below:

IX — THE HERMIT

Wheel of Fortune

Some traditional meanings: Destiny; unexpected luck or good fortune; success; the ups and downs of life.

One alternate meaning: "The king and queen are riding high, and don't realize the wheel is turning and they're about to slide off into the abyss. Overall I think it means that there's a great crash or catastrophe coming."

Another: "I see these legs disappearing at the lower right, and I worry about that person. Let's call him Charlie. Charlie's just been dumped off the wheel, and he's probably terrified, but he's about to make a soft landing and realize that what he most feared was not so terrible after all."

Another: "All these people were riding for a fall—one has already gone over the edge—but suddenly this huge hand came out of the mist and stopped the wheel just before the others went off. They've been saved, and it's probably going to make them rethink how they are spending their lives."

What does this card mean to you? Write your notes in the space below:

Justice

Some traditional meanings: Equity, truth, triumph of the deserving side in law; education; a balanced mind or personality.

One alternate meaning: "She reminds me of the High Priestess, with the pillars and cloth behind her, but she's much more judgmental. The scales of truth are out of balance, and unless you set things right, she's going to use that sword."

Another: "I believe that the drapery behind her is actually attached to the sword. She just has to whirl around to her right and she'll be gone behind there in an instant. Now you see her, now you don't. I guess that's like justice in the real world."

Another: "I'm obsessed with what's behind that curtain. She's guarding it, nobody may pass; so there's something amazing or at least valuable there. I think I'm a little angry at her, because I really want to see what's back there."

What does this card mean to you? Write your notes in the space below:

The Hanged Man

Some traditional meanings: Wisdom, trials, self-sacrifice, prophecy; suspended decisions, a pause; surrender to a Higher Power.

One alternate meaning: "Bandits have robbed this man and hung him up by his foot, and just left him there. But instead of moaning and yelling, he's totally calm, totally accepting. He is where he is, and he's got a very philosophical attitude about it."

Another: "This is a highly disciplined person, who hangs upside down every day to increase the blood supply to his brain. I'm sure he also practices yoga and does other exercises. He wants to stay at the peak of mental and physical condition."

Another: "I thought at first he might be a sacrificed savior figure, like Christ on the cross, or Odin on the ash tree. But he's got this sort of jester or trickster look to him, and I wonder if he's just messing with people's minds; like, 'If I hang here long enough, will you worship me?'"

What does this card mean to you? Write your notes in the space below:

What does this card mean to you? Write your notes in the space below:

Death

Some traditional meanings: End, mortality, destruction; great change or transformation; a change in consciousness; birth and renewal.

One alternate meaning: "The huge, beautiful flower is there, almost as though it's meant to lure you forward. Then you see the thorns, and the figure of Death behind it, and you realize that you've been tricked, and trapped."

Another: "The river in the background is so peaceful in the sunset. It draws me, like I could imagine just floating and drifting on it forever. But Death is there, and the white rose, which must symbolize life. I think you have to get through life and past death before you can have the peace of the river."

Another: "For me the key is that little yellow square. I think it's Death's cloak clasp. It took me a while, but then I recognized it as the Tattvic symbol for Earth. Then it hit me: death is about the Earth plane, it's about your body going into the earth and—that's all. Death is not this Cosmic Thing or the End, it's just a transition that we've all inflated out of all proportion. No big deal, your spirit keeps going."

What does this card mean to you? Write your notes in the space below:

Temperance

Some traditional meanings: Economy, moderation, frugality, wise management; harmony, cooperation, and coordination; imagined things are manifested.

One alternate meaning: "This angel is so intent on his work that he's not watching where he's going. He's just stepped into the pool and is about to get very wet. Can't walk and chew gum at the same time."

Another: "He seems to be on the planet, but if you look closely you see that he's actually floating above the pond, just dipping one foot in. Also the water he's pouring is flowing at an odd angle, like it's not subject to normal physical laws. He's in the world but not of it, a vision from a higher plane."

Another: "The water or whatever he's pouring represents divine energy. It flows into one cup, through him, and out the other cup. He's mastered being a conduit for the energy, channeling it but not blocking it, and it makes him very clear and powerful."

What does this card mean to you? Write your notes in the space below:

XIV — TEMPERANCE

The Devil

Some traditional meanings: Rage, violence, force; bondage to greed and material-ism, matter dominating spirit, sensation without understanding; black magick.

One alternate meaning: "I see danger. The whole card reminds me of a tattoo you might see on an outlaw biker's arm; it makes me think of wild and free, but reck-less, and maybe violent, men."

Another: "It's so scary, so malevolent, I wonder; could it be this really sweet young goat, dressed up to be scary for Halloween? Otherwise it's just too Hollywood horror-movie to seem real. Somebody's trying for high drama, and overdoing the effect."

Another: "Submission is the word that comes to mind. The devil-goat is very dark and ominous, but its head is almost bowed under the inverted pentagram. Perhaps he's the agent or tool for some stronger, more intelligent force."

What does this card mean to you? Write your notes in the space below:

The Tower

Some traditional meanings: Adversity, calamity, ruin, unforeseen catastrophe; selfish ambition overthrown; disruption, possibly followed by enlightenment.

One alternate meaning: "This tower is being struck by lightning, battered by waves, on fire—but it's still standing strong. Some people have been lost, but the building continues against all odds."

Another: "The two figures falling from the tower actually jumped. They got tired of all the storm and melodrama, so they dived into the sea, where I think they will be rescued by friendly dolphins."

Another: "It's time for the tower to be destroyed. It's probably been there for centuries, guarding the status quo long after things were due to change. Now Mother Nature has said, 'Enough!' and is going to sweep it all away, so a fresh start can be made."

What does this card mean to you? Write your notes in the space below:

The Star

Some traditional meanings: Hope, courage, and inspiration; bright prospects, health, spiritual love; help is coming. Another source says loss, theft, privation, abandonment.

One alternate meaning: "This card means absolute safety or security to me. The woman is outdoors at night, completely naked, and she's totally calm and peaceful. She knows she's in a safe place. I can't even imagine how that must feel."

Another: "There's a seven-pointed star right over her head. I've heard that's the sign of a special messenger. I think she's a divine messenger or maybe a new messiah sent to teach humanity. She's doing a ritual cleansing in preparation for her mission."

Another: "She seems to be up before dawn, rinsing out the jugs, maybe getting fresh water for the day. Perhaps she lives alone in a tiny cabin in the forest and communes with animals and birds, like Thoreau but less inhibited."

What does this card mean to you? Write your notes in the space below:

The Moon

Some traditional meanings: Imagination, intuition, dreams; hidden enemies, unforeseen danger to you or loved ones; deception, and error.

One alternate meaning: "It's a huge full moon, and the dogs are baying and the lobster has come out of the pond. There's going to be some kind of ancient ritual performed by all the animals, as they've done since the beginning of time, and no human will ever know about it."

Another: "Each dog is being a watch dog for one of the towers, and they're barking at each other across the boundary path. The lobster wants to be a mediator and make peace between the dogs and their families."

Another: "The lobster has this long journey ahead of it, and it wanted to travel by night because it thought it would be safer. But when it gets ready to leave, there are a dog and a wolf out there. So the lobster is frustrated; there are obstacles it didn't expect and it may have to delay its trip."

What does this card mean to you? Write your notes in the space below:

_____

_____

_____

_____

_____

_____

_____

_____

_____

_____

_____

XVIII — THE MOON

The Sun

Some traditional meanings: Material happiness; fortunate marriage; achievements in art, science, or agriculture; pleasure in the simple life; completion and contentment.

One alternate meaning: "They're in a walled garden, very warm and safe; but it's high noon and the sun's getting too warm. They are going to want to get past that wall and discover a wider world, with mountains and cool sea breezes."

Another: "Either the young woman and man are sister and brother, or they are two aspects of the same person, the feminine and masculine sides of a personality. Maybe this is the Sacred Marriage, where someone finally comes to terms with her 'other half' within."

Another: "The girl has stronger facial features. She's the leader, the guide, the initiator here. The boy will follow her lead."

What does this card mean to you? Write your notes in the space below:

Judgment

(Also called the Last Judgment)

Some traditional meanings: Change of position; total loss through lawsuit; a change in personal consciousness; renewal.

One alternate meaning: "There's all this excitement with the horn and bright colors, but the family is in deep shadow. There are great events happening over their heads, but as much as they wish they could be, they're not really involved."

Another: "Obviously these people have a wonderful dream or vision. It looks like they're floating across a lake, on their way to make it happen. They're very poor, have no clothes and not much of a boat, but they have great faith."

Another: "Here's this man lifting a fiery trumpet, like he's a herald of something glorious. The kid is excited but the woman just clutches herself like that wimpy '*Venus on the Half-Shell*' by Botticelli. I think it's a guy thing and she's wishing she could be someplace else."

What does this card mean to you? Write your notes in the space below:

The World

Some traditional meanings: Completion, success, triumph in all things; travel, a voyage, change of place; the achievement of cosmic consciousness.

One alternate meaning: "The woman is the center of her family's universe. They are all looking outward to opportunities and challenges in the wider world, but she's the one who holds everything together."

Another: "She's the Goddess, the cosmic dancer who manifests all things. Here she is symbolically creating animals, the plant world, and humanity."

Another: "It's as though she's coming through a gateway in time and space. Maybe she is me, my persona from past lives and distant places, coming to consciousness at last, making me whole."

What does this card mean to you? Write your notes in the space below:

_____

_____

_____

_____

_____

_____

_____

_____

_____

_____

_____

_____

_____

_____

Chapter 4

The Minor Arcana

The "pip cards" in the Minor Arcana of the first Tarot decks could not have been used for Gestalt Tarot; most querents who looked at a picture of three cups or seven wands would have had very little to stimulate the imagination, and would have had to rely on the reader's explanation of the official meaning of each card, or on the reader's intuitive guess about the meaning.

As we did with the Major Arcana, we will look at each card from at least four different perspectives, as four people might see them. This will provide a tiny sample of the infinite range of possible meanings. Not all of the Minor Arcana will be included, but just enough cards to get a feeling for the possibilities.

Note that in the *Morgan-Greer* deck, the Wands are called "Rods."

This time, try this exercise: before you read any of the suggested meanings, just look at the card and discover the story or meaning you see in it. Then, and only then, read what others might come up with.

The Queen of Swords

Some traditional meanings: A strong and capable woman. Also widowhood, separation, sterility, and mourning, female sadness in general. Clearly pre-Xena, the Warrior Princess.

One alternate meaning: "Here are these beautiful huge roses . . . it's an attractive, even alluring situation, but it conceals great danger. I feel like this queen is guarding something, warning me off. If I reach for one of those roses it's all over."

Another: "There's great sadness there, great pain. She's been terribly wounded in the past and nobody is going to get close enough to hurt her again."

Another: "She's looking into my eyes and judging whether I am worthy to hold the sword. It's like there is some great mission, some higher purpose waiting for a champion, and she's measuring whether I'm up to the task."

What does this card mean to you? Write your notes in the space below:

Six of Swords

Some traditional meanings: A smooth passage out of a difficult situation. Also a journey by water, an envoy, or expedience.

One alternate meaning: "I think the cloaked woman has been forced to leave her home, and is going to a new place that's very scary and threatening. All those swords make it feel like there's nothing but barriers and danger in front of her."

Another: "The man poling the boat is a blacksmith, and he's taking his swords to market across the river. There's a cold breeze across the water, but his wife is huddled in her warm cloak, sleepily daydreaming about the fabrics and ribbons she will buy, and the sweets for sale, and the music from wandering minstrels."

Another: "It's a secret mission. Definitely. These people are like commandos carrying weapons to a hidden rendezvous where they will meet other fighters who are plotting to overthrow the evil king."

What does this card mean to you? Write your notes in the space below:

Seven of Swords

Some traditional meanings: Coping with authority, with partial success. Also wishes, hopes, a confident attempt. Or quarreling, annoyance, a plan likely to fail.

One alternate meaning: "This guy's a thief. He's making off from a camp by the oasis, and he's got most of their swords. He would have grabbed them all but they're heavy, so he's only taking what he can carry."

Another: "A very brave man knows that a battle is brewing, and he believes that the conflict can be resolved peacefully, so he's taking all the weapons from both armies and hiding them. That will delay the war and maybe force them to negotiate."

Another: "I think this person is a sort of gofer. His job is to fetch and carry for the warriors; maybe he's a squire, but he's got a mature beard so he came to this job kind of late in life."

What does this card mean to you? Write your notes in the space below:

Ace of Rods

Some traditional meanings: The source of inspiration, creativity, and spiritual power. Invention and enterprise; money, fortune, or inheritance; virility, creation, birth, and family.

One alternate meaning: "There's a beautiful green forest below, and this hand is holding a chopped-off branch. It's a warning that unless we protect nature, the forests will be clear cut and destroyed."

Another: "Even though this stick has been cut, it's sprouting green leaves. It could be a sign of hope, that no matter what happens to us, something new can always grow."

Another: "It reminds me of *Macbeth*. The witches said he was safe 'til Birnam Wood shall come to Dunsinane,' which seemed impossible. Then the soldiers cut branches to camouflage themselves and came to the castle, so the prophecy was fulfilled and Macbeth was destroyed."

What does this card mean to you? Write your notes in the space below:

ACE OF RODS

Nine of Rods

Some traditional meanings: Prepared to meet the foe, boldness, strength, victory. Or delay, suspension, adjournment, a period of waiting.

One alternate meaning: "This knight is trying to get to the mountains, but this line of staves has magically sprung up to bar his path. He pulled one up and another just grew in its place, so he's trying to figure out some way to get past."

Another: "A soldier who used to be a simple woodsman is on his way to battle, but dreaming about his former life in the forest and wishing he could go back to who he was."

Another: "Here's an elite horseman in some ancient army, on his way to mount up. They haven't invented stirrups yet, so they vault into their saddles using these poles. It's very ingenious."

What does this card mean to you? Write your notes in the space below:

Ten of Rods

Some traditional meanings: Perseverance despite heavy burdens. Also loss of a lawsuit. Falsity, deceit, disguise; oppression, loss of fortune, failure.

One alternate meaning: "He's going to build a cottage out of sticks and mud, for his family and beloved. It sounds primitive, but by the time it's plastered and whitewashed, with a flower garden, it will be very cozy and charming."

Another: "This man is taking freshly cut quarterstaffs to his companions, so they can defend a bridge or something. He's a leader who provides the resources and trains the men so they can succeed."

Another: "I think this is a young woman—well, so she's muscular—who is taking the sticks to a women's community in the forest, and they're going to build a gateway and have some kind of wonderful procession and ceremony, maybe a coming-of-age rite for an older girl."

What does this card mean to you? Write your notes in the space below:

Page of Cups

Some traditional meanings: Birth, opportunity, new beginnings. Also a young man who wishes to serve, especially in business. News, a message; reflection, meditation.

One alternate meaning: "Well, she's listening to this fish. It must be a magic fish, and it's giving her information that she can use to succeed on a quest."

Another: "To me cups represent feelings and emotions, so I would say that the page is learning something about his emotions . . . maybe that they're not as scary as he thought, that it's okay to have strong emotions. Because, you see the fish isn't that scary, it's just a little blue fish."

Another: "All right, somebody put this fish in his wine for a joke. The page is looking at it and thinking, 'Okay, now what do I do?' Everybody at the table is watching him, and he wants to say something clever to show that he's not freaked, but he's got no clue."

What does this card mean to you? Write your notes in the space below:

PAGE OF CUPS

Three of Cups

Some traditional meanings: Abundance, contentment, happy outcome. Also victory, fulfillment, or healing.

One alternate meaning: "It's very festive. There's food and wine, and the women are all dressed up with flower garlands. I think that these three women are celebrating their friendship, a lifelong bond."

Another: "There's a blonde, and a redhead, and a brunette at a party. The bartender says, 'Would you ladies like any more wine?' The redhead and brunette say, 'Pretty soon, our glasses are half empty.' And the blonde says, 'That's funny, I've been drinking as much as you have and my cup is still half full.'"

Another: "They are fairies or elves or wood nymphs, and they live in a parallel world all around us, where life is filled with love and beauty and happiness. Our world is just skewed away from that, like we took a wrong turn somewhere; but if we just knew how, we could step across into that other world."

What does this card mean to you? Write your notes in the space below:

Nine of Cups

Some traditional meanings: Satisfaction, completion, contentment, well-being. Also victory, success, or advantage.

One alternate meaning: "This man's an avaricious pig. He's got all that wealth back there, all these golden goblets, and he's not sharing any of it. And he's got this self-satisfied smirk."

Another: "I guess it might be a bartender or innkeeper, with a prosperous tavern. He's this jolly, happy type and people love to come to his place because it's always cheerful there."

Another: "There's a choice being offered. This person is asking me to choose one of the chalices, and maybe it's got a healing potion in it, and all the rest just have ale or something that would make me drunk. He's smiling—it's not a nice smile— because he thinks I won't choose the right one."

What does this card mean to you? Write your notes in the space below:

Knight of Pentacles

Some traditional meanings: A competent, responsible person who has gained many skills in a lifetime of service. Also something useful and serviceable.

One alternate meaning: "The knight is about to go into battle, and he's really sweating it. I don't just mean the armor is hot. He's really worried about the outcome, and he feels trapped."

Another: "There's all this green leafy stuff on his helmet, he looks like an exploded can of spinach. Seriously, I think he's a really strong person, very powerful in combat, but he doesn't think much about what he's fighting for."

Another: "I'm noticing the red scarf tied on his arm, and thinking that it's a love token or favor from a lady who's waiting for him. No, not just waiting; she's a warrior too, fighting a battle far away, and he's concerned about her safety and not very focused on his own battle. Ooh, that could be dangerous."

What does this card mean to you? Write your notes in the space below:

Four of Pentacles

Some traditional meanings: Clinging to wealth and possessions to maintain one's own identity. Or gift, legacy, inheritance.

One alternate meaning: "Look at the design on the king's forehead, on his third eye chakra. This is a very psychic and spiritually powerful ruler, who uses his powers to keep his kingdom safe and prosperous."

Another: "This person has to take care of the discs, but his responsibilities blind him to the other important things in life. He's got a mental wall around him, and can't see past his immediate duties. I don't think he ever goes out for pizza."

Another: "This king has all this power, all this energy, but he hoards it. He's afraid to use it in case he might need it worse someday in the future, but in the meantime nothing gets done. I think the pentacles are just going to fade away unless he does something soon."

What does this card mean to you? Write your notes in the space below:

Eight of Pentacles

Some traditional meanings: Skilled craftsmanship, financial security. Also work or employment.

One alternate meaning: "This man is totally focused on his work. He's single-minded, and he's able to accomplish a huge amount because he will not let himself be distracted."

Another: "The guy feels like a fraud. He makes all these beautiful things and everybody loves them, but he's never satisfied with his own work. He sees every little flaw, even if nobody else notices."

Another: "The pentacles are magical protective shields, and he's making lots of them. He has something very, very important that he must protect, even if it takes a thousand of these things."

What does this card mean to you? Write your notes in the space below:

At this point it should be clear that any given card has potentially as many meanings as there are people in the world. A card reveals the personality, life issues, and questions of the person reflecting on it; or reflected in it, for it is really a kind of "magick mirror." All it takes to discover the individual, unique meaning of a particular card for a particular querent is patience, and encouragement in the form of nonleading questions.

The

Minor

Arcana

Chapter 5

The Gestalt
Tarot Spreads

The Gestalt system of reading the cards can be used with any spread. However, we were taught a particular spread to go with it, and we pass this on along with a shorter variation simply called the Condensed Gestalt Spread. These spreads can be placed on any surface, but for convenience you may want to draw the diagram of the spread on a cloth or board and place the cards on it during a reading. Chapter 6 explains in more detail how to make one of these.

The Planetary Correspondences

The traditional Gestalt Spread consists of twelve cards arranged as shown in the diagram on page 91. The positions are named and numbered as follows:

    I. THE SUN: Power Source.

    II. THE MOON: Emotional Position.

    III. EARTH: The Self.

    IV. JUPITER: Things in Your Favor.

    V. SATURN: Opposition or Teacher.

    VI. VENUS: Love, or The Female Principle.

    VII. MARS: Action, or The Male Principle.

    VIII. MERCURY: Message, Thought.

IX. NEPTUNE: Prophecy, The Future.

X. URANUS: Changes.

XI. VESTA: The Unknown Factor.

XII. PLUTO: Beginning, End, and Outer Boundary.

The Gestalt Tarot Spread

Let's examine each of the planetary correspondences in more depth.

I. THE SUN: Power Source

This represents the force that motivates or drives the querent at this time. It is not the only motivator, or even necessarily the most powerful in the long term. But it is the primary factor in regard to the particular question or focus of this reading.

All too many people work from unexamined motives. They may have an easy rationalization for why they behave as they do, but sometimes this is a face-saving or socially acceptable excuse for conduct that springs from deeper sources. How many times have we heard statements like "I did it for your own good," or "I didn't have any choice, others made me do it?" How rarely do we hear something honest and insightful like "I was afraid of losing control" or "I have to do a self-sacrifice thing in order to feel good about myself."

Knowing what motivates us allows us to understand our own actions better and make responsible choices.

II. THE MOON: Emotional Position

The card in this position may not capture the mood of the immediate moment, but rather the predominant emotion associated with the question or issue at hand. If it is an open-ended reading about the querent's life, the card summarizes how the querent has been feeling in general recently.

At first glance it seems an odd thing to include in a reading; after all, don't we know how we are feeling at any given moment, or about any given issue? Well, sometimes we don't. Many people in this society are raised to ignore their emotions, and be very task-oriented or outer-directed. And any of us can become so mentally focused, or so distracted, that we never pause to take a deep breath and ask, "How am I feeling?" This is especially true when emotions build gradually and insidiously over a long period, as when a minor irritant builds bit by bit to an explosion of anger. It may also occur when a chance comment pushes our buttons,

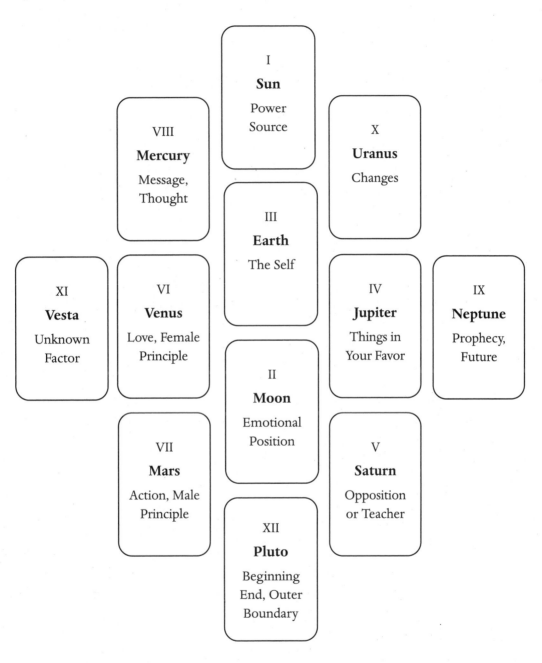

The Gestalt Tarot Spread

triggering old memories or reactions which have nothing to do with the present situation, and everything to do with personal past history.

All of this might be moot if we had no control over our feelings. But we have. The whole basis of Gestalt Tarot is self-understanding *and empowerment*, the belief that we can do something about our lives; and that includes our emotions.

By "controlling emotions" we do not mean denying them, "stuffing" them, or letting them run riot internally while we rigidly control our external behavior. Emotions can be handled by acknowledging them, understanding their source, and making conscious choices about what to do about them. We change our emotions by choosing what to think about, by reframing events or looking at them from a new perspective, or by immersing ourselves in them instead of trying to avoid them. We can take the energy of negative emotions and channel it toward constructive ends (like finding a better job), or at least harmless ones (like playing golf). In all of these, the very first step is to honestly look at our feelings.

III. EARTH: The Self

We are all many selves. In a single day one woman may play the roles of Mother, Wife, Executive, Artist, Friend, Driver, and Party Girl. Sometimes one role looms large in our lives; circumstances demand that we live it more deeply, intensely, thoroughly, as our other faces recede into shadow for the moment.

The Earth card shows the querent which role—which self—is pre-eminent in a certain situation, or at this time in life. Like all the cards, it is a mirror reflecting the querent's life, but this one is a summation of who they are, here and now.

The querent may or may not like the reflection, but must seek the truth of it, must acknowledge its reality. Then they can choose whether to continue playing that role, or to select another facet of their myriad Self to play out, and so alter the destiny that lies ahead.

IV. JUPITER: Things In Your Favor

The Jupiter card symbolizes a person, event, or force that is helping the querent, or available to help if the querent is open to the possibility. Now "help" is a slippery term. We may not always be helped toward comfort, ease, immediate happiness, or any of the other goodies we crave. The card's referent may help us toward what is necessary for survival, or toward a long-term goal along a path that is difficult or even painful.

This explains why "negative" cards occasionally turn up here; cards that appear filled with gloom, loss, despair, or bloodshed. Real life includes all these things. However, as older and wiser heads may realize, sometimes difficult or tragic stuff leads to some positive results. A love relationship falls apart, and a year later we meet someone far more compatible. An illness forces us to slow down, rethink our lifestyle, and make some better choices.

All we can be sure of is that the end result will be beneficial in the context of the reading's key question.

When "happy" cards appear in this position, it is tempting to say, "Oh that's nice," and move on after a superficial glance. Resist the urge; explore the card thoroughly until you find the deeper meaning. What exactly is working in the querent's favor, and how can it be utilized, maintained, or even strengthened?

V. SATURN: Opposition or Teacher

The Saturn card can be as complex as the card in the Jupiter position. It does represent an obstacle, something in opposition to the querent's progress or immediate success. However, it can also be the teacher, or the barrier we overcome that makes us stronger as we labor to get past it. Think of the high-school teacher who was stern and demanding and generally disliked by students; yet years later, you remember more from his class than any other. Think of the military drill instructor who drove you almost past endurance—and made you tougher.

So think of this card not necessarily as unmitigated bother, without redeeming value. If the querent can get past it, it may make success all the sweeter.

In a mirror of the Jupiter phenomenon, you may see sweetness-and-light cards turn up that actually prove to be a huge problem. The "helpful" friend who inadvertently makes a situation worse; the newfound wealth that causes more headaches than it solves; the prestigious position that takes so much time and energy that your real desires get sidetracked—there are a lot of ways that a stroke of apparent good fortune can mess up your plans.

Look carefully at the Saturn card. If it looks great, be suspicious; and if it seems terrible, discover what lessons you can learn in surviving it.

VI. VENUS: Love, or The Female Principle

The Venus card may refer to a loving relationship; to the querent's relationships in general; to a female who has an important role in the issue or question at hand; the querent's capacity to love; or the feminine, receptive, sensitive side of their personality.

The card in this position may give you an immediate idea of which of these alternatives is relevant. If the card has two or more people in it, it's a good bet that relationships are at issue. A card with one figure might refer to your attitude or approach to relationships, but could equally well refer to a woman with an important role in the situation.

If you cannot discover a link to relationships or to an individual, then consider the possibility that the card symbolizes the feminine side of your personality, or your capacity for love.

VII. MARS: Action, or The Male Principle

The card in the Mars position usually refers to some action that the querent has just taken, or is contemplating, or should consider. This can be very useful to the action-oriented, decisive individual who wants to know "But what should I *do*?" (Or "Did I do the right thing?")

However, the card can also refer to a man or boy who is a key player in the situation being explored. The identity of the figure may be revealed quite blatantly by his appearance, or more subtly by his posture, expression, or what he is doing. If it does refer to a certain individual, you may be certain that some clue in the card will tell you who it is.

On rare occasions, the card may speak to the masculine side of the querent's personality—if that has a bearing on the question originally asked. For example, suppose that the whole reading is about a relationship. In the Mars position, the querent places the Eight of Cups, which depicts a cloaked figure walking away from a stack of chalices. This could refer to some men's tendency to be uncomfortable with intense emotion, and to turn away from any situation where emotion is expressed or expected. If this applies to the querent's personality, it has some pretty obvious ramifications for any close relationship in which they are involved.

VIII. MERCURY: Message, Thought

The god Mercury is the patron of communications, among other things, and the card in this position may be considered to be a "telegram from the Deep Mind" of the querent. It is a message of great importance from the subconscious, which retains information and develops insights not easily available to the conscious, rational mind. It may clarify a vague intuition or instinct that the querent has felt, but has never been able to put into words before.

On rare occasions, it may also refer to the querent's ability to communicate, or style of communication, as these impact the original question.

IX. NEPTUNE: Prophecy, The Future

The card in the Neptune position provides the closest thing in a Gestalt reading to "fortunetelling." It does actually show the answer to the querent's question, or the outcome of the situation, *providing that the querent and other key players continue the same pattern of behavior.*

Thus the Tarot can help extrapolate trends into the future, just as one could find a driver's destination by projecting their current direction across a highway map—assuming they don't turn off before they reach the city in front of them.

The querent must be made to understand that the Neptune card represents only the most likely outcome, assuming nobody involved does anything very different. If the querent is unhappy with the outcome shown, all they have to do is change their behavior and a new outcome replaces it. If the big green sign over the highway says "CLEVELAND STRAIGHT AHEAD," and you don't want to go to Cleveland, then take the first exit and go someplace else.

Very little is preordained, immutable destiny. All human beings bear responsibility for their own lives, and can decide to change them. Tarot can lift the veil a little so that people can make informed decisions as to whether they want to continue on to the destinations before them, or choose new directions.

Very little is preordained, immutable destiny. All human beings bear responsibility for their own lives, and can decide to change them. Tarot can lift the veil a little so that people can make informed decisions as to whether they want to continue on to the destinations before them, or choose new directions.

X. URANUS: Changes

The Uranus card can show a major change that has just taken place (of which the querent may or may not be aware), or a change that is about to happen.

If the change has already occurred, then the card's purpose is either to bring it to the querent's attention, or to confirm its existence and clarify its nature.

If the change is about to occur and is a negative one, this may be the querent's last chance to avoid it or, at least, prepare for it. If the coming change is positive, the querent may be heartened and face the situation with more confidence and optimism.

XI. VESTA: The Unknown Factor

In case it has not been made clear that the future is mutable, we have the Vesta position to remind us. The Vesta card depicts the person, event, or decision that could change the entire direction of the reading. It may represent a potential stroke of serendipity, unforeseen luck, the prince (or princess) on the white horse who dashes up to save your bacon.

Equally possibly, the Vesta card can depict the monkey wrench in the works, the bureaucratic snag that brings a screeching halt to your plans, the planned superhighway that gets rerouted through your yard.

In either case, good or bad, it shows an uncertainty factor. It balances on the cusp, may be shifted by a breath or a whim, and may or may not come to pass. The card is worth exploring because it has the potential to change everything. If you can identify the Vesta factor, a small action on your part may avert a catastrophe or ensure a victory.

XII. PLUTO: Beginning, End, and Outer Boundary.

The Pluto position exists to provide perspective on the entire situation.

Because the querent is intimately involved, it is difficult to stand back and see where it all started, what the Big Issue is, what defines the whole problem. Understanding the Pluto card is like looking at the solar system from its outermost planet, seeing its shape and pattern clearly without the contours of the Earth and the glare of the sun in your face.

If the reading is about a relationship, Pluto shows the key dynamic that defines how the two people interact. If it is about a career, Pluto explains what the whole idea of career means to the individual. If it is a general life reading, Pluto sums up the paradigm by which the person understands existence and deals with life's challenges. The Pluto card is the bottom line context in which everything else makes sense.

The message of the Pluto card is not always easy to perceive and understand, any more than we pay attention to the air we breathe or a fish notices the water in which it swims. But the effort is worth it, because understanding Pluto allows the querent to redirect the whole situation, and perhaps their entire life.

Understanding Patterns in the Spread

During the reading, the cards will not just be interpreted singly. They will also form patterns that the reader can bring to the querent's attention (Note that the reader may reveal the pattern, but must leave interpretation up to the querent.) Here are some patterns you may find:

The Order in Which the Cards Are Placed

As the querent places the cards face-down on the spread, make a mental note of which positions they fill first. It has been suggested that this may reflect the querent's subconscious priorities. For example, filling the Venus position first might mean that the querent is more concerned about a relationship than anything else, even if they have consciously stated that the reading is about a career choice or something else.

A querent who fills the Sun position first may subconsciously be feeling helpless or out of control; one who fills the Earth position first may be struggling with identity issues; filling the Moon position early suggests emotional turmoil; and so on.

You can bring this up with a comment such as: "Your subconscious or deep mind chose the order in which you placed the cards at the beginning. Why do you suppose you filled the Moon position first?"

The Order in Which the Cards Are Revealed

When the querent turns the cards over one at a time, they may be revealing their conscious priorities and concerns. For example, the querent who turns the Neptune (future) card first is apprehensive about how everything will turn out; they want to cut to the chase and see if there's a happy ending.

On the other hand, the turning of the cards may gradually reveal a storyline progression. For example, a Knight is revealed, then a cloaked figure walking away from some spilled cups, then a scene showing conflict or struggle, then a Page, then two figures standing close together in a castle. The storyline might be as follows: the querent (Knight) suffers some emotional loss and goes away on a journey, struggles with their feelings, meets someone (the Page) and forms a new relationship, and together they build a new home and life.

Not all stories will be so simple and easy to follow; and it may take some real delving to find the storyline. However, once you understand the beginning the rest usually falls into place. Remember, however, that you may suggest that a story is hidden in the cards, but it must be the querent who actually tells the story.

The Story Told in a Pattern on the Board

The cards may tell a story, but it may not appear in chronological order as the cards are turned over. Instead, the story may be seen after all the cards are revealed, for example moving from the querent's left to right across the spread, or spiraling out from the center, or in some other order.

Upper and Lower Halves

Cards in the upper half of the spread can reveal the outward events and the querent's conscious thoughts about them; cards in the lower half may allow you to explore underlying causes, deeper meanings, and subconscious feelings and desires.

Resist the temptation to play Sigmund Freud if this pattern starts to emerge. Your job as reader is not, repeat *not*, to psychoanalyze the querent. Your job is to ask a lot of neutral questions and let the querent find their own meanings. Here are some examples of questions that might be appropriate for this pattern:

(Pointing to the card in the Moon position) "So how is this person feeling about the situation? How do you feel about your own situation? Any parallels or contrasts in your emotions? Take a moment to silently examine your feelings, and see if there's anything else there."

(Pointing to the card in the Pluto position) "Where do you think this whole situation started? What's the cause? And what caused that? If you were going to sum it up, tell us the bottom line in one sentence, what would it be? Finish this sentence: 'It's really all about _____.'"

The Proportion of Major to Minor Arcana

Most readings will include a mixture of Major and Minor Arcana. There are seventy-eight cards in a standard deck, and twenty-two are Major Arcana, so on the average you can expect three or four cards in a Gestalt Spread will be Major Arcana.

A tradition exists that if all (or mostly) Minor Arcana turn up, it means the topic of the reading is pretty humdrum in the scheme of the querent's whole life. If the topic of the reading is the querent's whole life, then Minor Arcana would indicate that this is not a time of significant change; it's business as usual, at least for the immediate future.

What if mostly Major Arcana turn up? Then the question is, in theory, deeply important to the querent's life and future; the querent may be at a decision-making cusp that will change everything.

You may wish to take this whole theory with a grain of salt. We do, because we don't know of any mechanism to make it work. However, it may be useful in forcing the querent to ask, "How important is this whole question anyway?" Are they making mountains out of molehills? Conversely, is a seemingly ordinary question more important that it looked at first glance?

Asking the question will help the querent put the issue in perspective.

Abundance or Scarcity of Court Cards

Similarly, the proportion of court cards (Kings, Queens, Knights, and Pages) can have some meaning. There are sixteen court cards in a seventy-eight-card deck, so you would expect an average of two or three in each Gestalt reading.

The querent must decide what, if anything, a low or high proportion means. You can suggest that it is another potential field of meaning; for example:

"I notice that there are a lot of Kings and Queens here; what are some words you associate with royalty? How might they apply to this question?"

Or: "We seem to have turned up all four Pages. What do you think of when you look at the Pages? Do you ever feel like that? How about in this situation?"

Take care not to force the querent into an association that isn't really important to them. If it doesn't come fairly quickly, move on, and find a pattern more significant to the querent.

The Proportions of the Four Suits

Although a Gestalt Spread would be expected on the average to have three of each suit represented, usually one suit (Wands, Swords, Cups, or Pentacles) will show up more than the others in a spread. Occasionally two suits will be more numerous than the other two, or one suit may be entirely absent.

Your job as reader is to draw the querent's attention to the balance or imbalance of suits, and help them find their meaning for that pattern. If the querent seems stuck, you can remind them of the traditional correspondences for the suits, and see if that clicks for them. For example, "We've noticed that there are a lot of Swords showing up in this spread. In some systems, Swords are associated with the element of Fire, which can refer to energy, will, driving toward a goal, or passion. What do you think it means that you have so many Swords here?"

Supposing the querent just looks blank. You can ask further how this reading related to their energy, or *lack of energy* . . . their will, *or lack of will* . . . their goals, *or lack of goals* . . . or their passion, *or lack of passion*. In other words, is the preponderance of Swords referring to something that is abundant in the querent's life, or something that is sorely lacking, but necessary if they are to achieve balance?

In the case of Swords or Wands, there may be an additional complication in that not all schools agree on their traditional meanings. In some traditions, Wands represent Fire (energy, will, passion) and Swords represent Air (mind, intellect, thought, ideas, imagination). This is how they are represented in the Morgan-Greer deck we have been using, and in the Rider-Waite deck from which it derives.

So if the Swords / Fire correlation rings no bells for the querent, you can always add, "In some traditions Swords represent Air, which stands for ideas, beliefs, or imagination. How do your beliefs affect the situation we are exploring with this spread? What are you imagining, or what might you imagine, that would change the outcome?" And so on. With Swords and Wands, you have not one but two traditional springboards in the search for meaning.

The traditional meanings for Cups and Pentacles are more firmly established. Commonly, Cups represent the Element of Water, and emotions, feelings, or intuition. Pentacles symbolize the Element of Earth, and our bodies, possessions, wealth, and all material things; they can also represent foundations or basic principles.

Of course, the traditional correspondences may not have any meaning for the querent at all. That is why you, the reader, should not even bring them up unless the querent is getting nowhere finding their own connections; then you can use the traditional correspondences to nudge the querent. Their response may be positive ("Oh yes, I see . . .") or negative ("Gee, that's not what Swords meant to me . . ."), but at least they will be on the move again.

Recurring Themes

Any number of design elements can turn up over and over in a spread. Watch for the frequent appearance of themes of any kind. These might include:

- Colors ("Notice that every card seems to have a lot of red in it")

- Objects ("Most of the figures are holding a staff or scepter")

- Animals ("There's yet another dragon on this card")

- Natural elements ("Why do you suppose there's always water")

- Conflict or harmony ("So we've seen some sort of struggle between people in several cards")

- Lone figures vs. pairs vs. groups ("Every card has shown one solitary figure")

- Emotional themes ("So you're saying that each of these figures is feeling lonely")

These can be things that are inherent in the cards, such as a color or animal, or they can be subjective elements that the querent sees in every card where others might not, such as purposes or emotions. In either case, watch for patterns, watch for themes, but let the querent assign the meaning.

The Condensed Spread:
A Short Version

The Condensed Spread is similar to the full Gestalt Spread, but focuses on a few basic areas and can be done much more quickly. It consists of six cards arranged as shown in the accompanying diagram (p. 102). The positions are named and numbered as follows:

    I. EARTH: The self.

    II. PLUTO: The situation.

    III. SATURN: Opposition or teacher.

    IV. JUPITER: Things in your favor.

    V. MERCURY: Guidance.

    VI. NEPTUNE: Prophecy, the future.

    The Earth card is in the center, with Pluto to the lower right, Saturn to the lower left, Jupiter to the upper left, and Neptune to the upper right. The Mercury card is laid across the Earth card. (See the accompanying diagram.)

The Process

The Condensed Spread is handled exactly like the full twelve-card Gestalt Spread. That is, the querent shuffles the deck, places cards face-down in each position, then turns them over one at a time and interprets them with the reader's help. However, rather than use your usual cloth or board for this layout, you may want to create another one specifically for the Condensed Spread.

When to Use the Condensed Spread

    The short version is appropriate whenever you simply don't have time for a more thorough reading. The full spread can easily take two hours for an in-depth exploration, whereas the Condensed Spread can be done in less than an hour if necessary. If it takes less than forty-five minutes, it may mean either that (a) you have a very laconic querent, or (b) you are moving too fast and suggesting or forcing interpretations.

    Of course with this spread, the querent is simply not going to get as much information or understanding—and superficial understanding may lead to less-than-optimal decisions and choices. So use this spread only where there is a genuine time crunch.

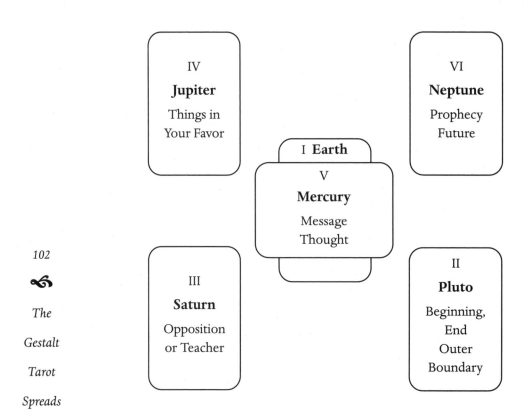

The Condensed Gestalt Spread

Some querents may be perfectly happy with a quick "tell me what to do" reading; but if you give them one, be aware that you are not helping the querent to become a stronger person, but taking responsibility for some of their life choices. Such clients really want a parent or an advice columnist, not self-insight and personal responsibility.

Summary

The spread, layout, or pattern of the cards is just as important as the meanings attributed to each individual card. Without a pattern, the querent is left with a series of isolated snapshots or postcards; each perhaps valuable by itself, but with no overview or broad perspective of the issue. The value of Tarot is that it can provide new insights, a different perspective, or deeper understanding to the querent. The spread is an important tool in doing this.

Section II

᪥ | ᪥

Reading with the
Gestalt Method

Chapter 6

Ԍecting Scarced
With Ԍestalt

Choosing a Tarot deck for Gestalt readings can be a lot of fun. Dozens of Tarot decks are on the market today, and more appear every year. The largest single source for decks is U.S. Games Systems, which publishes a catalog with many styles. Llewellyn Worldwide also has several new and beautiful designs. Perhaps some of your friends have decks you could look at, or there may be a metaphysical store in your area that stocks several varieties.

Here we will touch on some of the most popular designs:

The *Rider-Waite* deck (U.S. Games Systems, AGMüller), illustrated by Pamela Colman Smith, has been the standard since its release in 1910. Today the artwork seems a little quaint, reminiscent of illustrations in nineteenth-century English children's books. However, it set the pattern for many decks to follow, and is still one of the most popular designs around.

The *Morgan-Greer* deck (U.S. Games Systems), used in this book to illustrate the Gestalt Tarot, is firmly based on the *Rider-Waite* but has a bolder, more modern style of illustration, and its bold colors and evocative scenes are perfect for Gestalt readings. Like its predecessor, it is very colorful, and the structure is exactly the same, but the illustrations have a closer focus (larger figures) and are a little less detailed and busy.

The *Crowley Thoth Tarot* (U.S. Games Systems) is based on Aleister Crowley's famous magickal work, *The Book of Thoth*. It has some differences from the *Rider-Waite* pattern: the court cards include Queens,

Knights, Princes, and Princesses. The Major Arcana include such titles as The Aeon (Judgment), Adjustment (Justice), The Universe (World), Art (Temperance), and Lust (Strength); each is marked with a corresponding Hebrew letter and zodiac or planetary sign. The pip cards each have a title, such as Swiftness, Abundance, Power, Luxury, or Valor. The illustrations by Lady Frieda Harris are powerful and sometimes startling.

The *Aquarian Tarot* by David Palladini (Morgan Press) has more delicate pictures, done in an art deco style, and uses a lot of pastels. It is quite well designed and beautiful—especially the costumes—but some of the design elements in earlier decks are not present so there are fewer symbols to work with for Gestalt Tarot.

The *Robin Wood Tarot* (Llewellyn) has excellent illustrations, updated symbolism, and bright colors, and has deservedly been called "vibrant" and "luminous." Those who do not relate well to the medieval, sometimes gloomy illustrations of earlier decks will enjoy this one; and there is a Spanish version available.

Many feminists prefer one of the multicultural circular decks. Perhaps the best known is *Motherpeace* (U.S. Games Systems); the artwork is primitive but the symbolism is evocative, done from a Goddess perspective, very Earth-based and woman-oriented. Both this and the following deck avoid the rather hierarchical and patriarchal King-Queen-Knight-Page format of some of the older decks.

Daughters of the Moon Tarot (Daughters of the Moon) is another round deck, well drawn but in black-and-white line drawings. Coloring each card becomes a meditation in which you can reflect on its meaning and connect more strongly to the deck. You can have a party and invite your friends to each color a few cards, thus filling the deck with the energies of the people closest to you.

The *Voyager Tarot* (U.S. Games systems) is unlike any other Tarot deck. Its images are visually exciting montages of painting and photography, in evocative, almost abstract, combinations. It has no Major or Minor Arcana, but rather each card is named for a human experience. Sometimes the relation between the name and the image are obvious, sometimes they are very subtle.

The *Tarot of the Old Path* (AGMüller) by Sylvia Gainsford and Howard Rodway is more Wiccan in orientation than most. Cauldrons replace the suit of cups, and some of the cards have new titles such as Mastery (Chariot), Illusion (Moon), The High Priest (Pope or Hierophant), The Wise One (Hermit), The Lone Man (Hanged Man), The Close (Death), The Guide (Temperance), Temptation (Devil), and Karma (Judgment). The illustrations are light and bright and include the symbolism of flowers.

The *Golden Dawn Magical Tarot* (Llewellyn) was painted by Sandra Tabatha Cicero, an Adept of the Hermetic Order of the Golden Dawn. It features the

Golden Dawn "flashing colors," Hebrew letters, planetary and zodiacal symbols for each card, and the Qabalistic color scales. The court cards include Kings, Queens, Princes and Princesses. The illustrations are simple and very colorful.

The *Swiss 1JJ Deck* was originally published in 1865 from woodblocks cut by Johann Georg Rauch in Switzerland. (A newer, less crude version is now published by AGMüller & Cie, also of Switzerland.) The "JJ" in the title stands for Jupiter and Juno, who replace the Pope/Hierophant and Popess/High Priestess cards, perhaps to make the deck more acceptable to the Catholic Church. The titles are in French and the Minor Arcana are in the early form, with pip cards that show only the requisite number of Swords, Batons, Cups, and Coins. Because the pip cards have no other symbols, much less human figures or landscapes, these cards are difficult to use with the Gestalt method.

The *Visconti Sforza Tarocchi Deck* (U.S. Games Systems) originally dated from about 1430, so it is one of the earliest decks. It was commissioned by the Duke of Milan, possibly for a wedding. The cards are very large, have no numbers or titles, and are richly illustrated with lots of gold leaf. Since four of the original cards are lost, the version reprinted by U.S. Games Systems includes some very well-done replacements.

The *Fantasy Showcase Tarot* (Morgan Press, U.S. Games Systems), organized by Bruce Pelz, is fascinating in that eighty-five different fantasy illustrators each created a card; some of the new cards include Separation and The Farrier as trumps, and the addition of four Ladies to the court cards. The styles vary incredibly from primitive cartoons to richly baroque art to science fiction-ish illustrations. Though hard to find, this Tarot is perhaps the most purely fun of any deck ever created; and yes, it works for Gestalt Tarot.

Some of the new decks published by Llewellyn are beautifully illustrated and very creative in their design. *The Celtic Dragon Tarot* by D. J. Conway and Lisa Hunt and the *Faery Wicca* deck by Kisma Stepanich and Renée Yates are two examples, and there are several others.

Many, many other decks are available on the market, some of them beautiful and some just rather odd. You can choose a Mayan deck where all the cards fit together to make one great frieze, several decks with Egyptian-theme designs; the *Tarot of the Cat People* with a science-fiction flavor and large alien felines on every card; the *Rock Art Tarot* based on Southwestern petroglyphs; the *Dragon Tarot*; or the *Crow's Magick Tarot* for those who enjoy black birds, and many more.

If you are bewildered by the variety of choices, you can always start with the *Rider-Waite* deck, which has been a sort of standard for nearly a century. Each card is full of detail and symbolism, so there is no lack of raw material to use in a

Gestalt reading. My personal preference is usually the *Morgan-Greer* deck, which is the one used to illustrate this book. Because it has somewhat less detail than the *Rider-Waite*, it is easier to get through a reading in less than two or three hours.

Of course the bottom line is going to be: what works for the querent? If you are reading for yourself, you can just choose your personal favorite or you can switch decks occasionally so that certain meanings don't get fixed in your mind, and you approach each reading with a fresh perspective. Decks based on ancient cultures (Mayan, Egyptian, Old Norse, Italian Renaissance, early Native American, etc.) may not work for a given individual, unless the deck reflects their ancestry and they have an interest in their cultural roots. Likewise, a really avant-garde deck may not speak to most people. Some querents may bring along their own favorite deck, which will be comfortable and familiar. When reading for everyone else, just choose a deck with a style that is not too foreign to them.

A Taroc Cloth or Board

Another way of empowering the querent is to allow them to see what the various positions in the spread stand for. This can be done in several ways. You could simply photocopy the spread diagram you will be using from this book (see chapter 5, "The Gestalt Spreads"), and have it sitting on the table for the querent to look at.

More elegant and less distracting is to create a cloth or board with the full-size spread diagram on it, and ask the querent to actually place the cards on the diagram as you proceed. Making it will help you get acquainted with the spread design; during a reading the querent can easily place the cards in their correct pattern, and you can go to work without having to remember the meaning of every position.

Using a regular deck in which the cards are 2.75" x 4.75", such as the *Rider-Waite* or *Morgan-Greer*, you can fit the entire spread on a cloth or board about 19" x 24". This allows a little space between the cards and 1.5" of margin or border around the edges. If your deck is an unusual size, you can proportion the material accordingly.

For a Tarot cloth, purchase two-thirds of a yard of fabric and draw the diagram with fabric paints. The fabric should be nonshrinking or preshrunk; or if it contains cotton or anything else shrinkable, wash and iron it, then hem it, before you do your artwork. Then if you spill something on it later and have to wash it again, it won't shrivel and die.

Choose either a solid color fabric or something with a very subtle print that's not going to make it hard to read the diagram painted over it. It's best to choose a cool, subdued color, possibly a blue, green, or violet. Hot or bright colors may slightly affect the querent's emotional state and bias the reading.

When you purchase the fabric paint, make sure the color contrasts sharply with the fabric. Hobby shops carry special paint that comes in squeeze containers with narrow tips, so that you can draw with the tube rather than using a brush. Unless you are a skilled freehand artist, you will probably want to draw the diagram with pencil first and then trace over the lines with the paint.

Another alternative is to draw the diagram on a large sheet of paper in marker, ink, or paint; and then glue or decoupage the paper on to a sheet of Masonite. Masonite is a wood product, a thin, stiff board available at lumberyards and home-supply stores. You could use a sheet of illustration board from an art supply shop, but Masonite is sturdier.

For paper you might use a large sheet of imitation parchment from the art shop or a printer. Real parchment is made from sheepskin or goatskin, and it seems unnecessary to use it when there are alternatives that work perfectly well.

Decoupage paste can be found in crafts and hobby stores or the art supply shop. Test it over your ink or whatever, on a scrap of paper, before you draw the whole diagram. You don't want to discover too late that the decoupage paste makes the ink run.

Of course, not everyone is an artist; but almost everyone knows an artist, or at least someone who can draw a straight line and letter fairly well. If the project seems too daunting, it's time to ask a graphically talented friend to help.

A Tarot Journal

If you read primarily for yourself, you may want to keep track of your readings in a journal. You can use a three-ring looseleaf binder, a blank composition book from a college bookstore or stationary shop, a diary, or a leather-bound journal from a metaphysical store. Make sure you put the date and question explored at the top of your notes for each reading. Each time you finish a new reading on a given topic, you may want to go back and review earlier readings on the same issue in order to learn what has changed.

Learning to See Your Tarot Deck Through Gestalt Eyes

Once you are set up with a deck, journal, and reading board if desired, begin some exercises to help you learn the Gestalt method. Here are five possibilities:

Exercise 1: Describe the action on each card in at least five different ways. Write down the descriptions. If any of them are quite similar, come up with another, completely different, description.

Exercise 2: Have five friends each give you their description of several cards and compare their descriptions to your own.

Exercise 3: Write a series of questions for each card that would help a querent describe the action, emphasizing nonleading questions (see chapter 8).

Exercise 4: Do at least five readings for yourself, on separate days (see chapter 7).

Exercise 5: Do at least five readings for the same friends who gave you their descriptions of the cards.

By doing these exercises, especially Exercise 1, you will begin to allow yourself to come to the cards fresh each time you do a reading, whether it is for yourself or for others. The goal here is to allow yourself to see the cards with unbiased eyes, and allow your querents to believe in their own descriptions of the cards, without any preconceived idea about what the cards should mean.

Chapter 7

Reading for Yourself

Gestalt Tarot can be used for your own personal guidance, but reading for yourself has its own set of challenges. This chapter is designed to help you get into the proper frame of mind, formulate your question, choose a technique that works for you and the situation, and avoid some of the pitfalls you might encounter along the way.

A Proper Mindset

You will be most likely to find useful answers if you can go into the reading in a calm and confident mood, then focus your attention on the issue at hand. Never attempt a reading when you are emotionally upset. Of course it is at times of emotional crisis that you may be most in need of guidance, but then it is generally wise to get a reading from someone you trust who is not in the middle of the situation.

If you feel you are calm enough to do the reading on your own, then begin with these steps:

- **Relax.** Close your eyes and check internally for tension. If necessary, do some activity you find relaxing; this could be anything from needlepoint to tai chi, gardening, artwork, carpentry, playing music, or yoga. You know best what relaxes you. If you can't think of anything else, then just do some slow stretching exercises and deep breathing, while you think of something pleasant.

- **Find Privacy.** Look for a quiet place where you will not be interrupted. This could be your bedroom, which ideally is already associated in your deep mind with privacy, safety, and relaxation. Or you might choose a study, den, or sewing room, if you have one. If the weather is good and you have a favorite spot outdoors that is secluded, try going there.

- **Ground.** This involves making a deep connection with the Earth. You can sit cross-legged on the floor or the ground and visualize a channel of energy reaching from deep in the earth to the top of your head. Then breathe out any tension you feel, and as you breathe in, draw up energy from the planet. You might visualize the energy as a vibrant green, a golden yellow, or a clear russet brown. You can also perform grounding by simply lying full-length on the ground and breathing slowly; by holding a large rock and breathing slowly; or by eating a solid meal (such as protein and root vegetables; no sugar or caffeine, please).

- **Center.** Once you have established your Earth link, then find your own center. Most of us go through daily life slightly off-balance in a spiritual, psychic, and emotional sense. You will need to go inside your own heart and mind to find that space where you feel calm, safe, and in harmony with yourself and the world. It may help to visualize yourself as a large house, with rooms corresponding to your different roles and activities; at the core of the house is a very safe, very quiet, very comfortable place that is totally your own. There in the strong, stable place at the center of your being, you will know that you are eternal, and will see all the problems of your life in their proper perspective.

- **Release Your Preconceptions.** You must approach your question and the Tarot cards with a fresh mind. Often when we face a personal problem, we allow ourselves to get locked into a set of assumptions that limit our choices. For example, if we have an argument with a friend, in confusion and despair we may see only two choices: end the relationship or give in. Yet life is rarely that black-and-white. You have other options. Give it a rest while you both think about the issue calmly. Ask a counselor or wise friend for advice. Agree to disagree. Look for a win-win answer that will eliminate the argument by giving you each what you need. Find a mediator who will facilitate the discussion. Turn the issue over to an arbitrator, a respected mutual acquaintance who will make a binding decision. Whatever the question you bring to the Tarot reading, drop your assumptions and open yourself to creative new possibilities.

Then there are the Tarot cards. If you have been trained in traditional Tarot, where each card has a set meaning, you will need to let go of all those ideas and look at the cards with fresh eyes. This can be difficult. Perhaps you have been taught that the Tower card means disaster or cataclysmic change. Can you release that idea, and see what the Tower has to say to you at this moment, on this issue? Maybe the lightning is knocking thieves off the tower before they can break into your home. Maybe the flames are a beacon, set deliberately. Maybe you and a companion are diving into the water for the sheer joy of it, and will meet friendly dolphins there. Look at the cards as though you have never seen them before, and know nothing of their traditional meanings.

Asking the Right Questions

Once you are mentally and emotionally prepared, you must frame your question for the reading. If you have no specific issue to bring to the cards, that's fine; ask a general sort of question such as, "What guidance can I find in the Tarot right now, to help me live today in wisdom, love, and strength?"

If you have a more specific concern, remember that Gestalt Tarot is not designed for "yes or no" questions. It works best when you want to understand the whole situation surrounding your issue—the "gestalt"—and all the influences and implications. Gestalt Tarot is expansive and wholistic by its very nature. So don't ask the cards, "*Should* I date Terence?" or, "*Should* I invest in technology stocks?" The Tarot won't tell you what you should do; that's your decision. It can only tell you what's likely to happen if you choose a certain course of action.

Phrase your questions more like this: "What are the energies surrounding a relationship between me and Terence?" or "What is the probable outcome if I invest in technology stocks?"

Then put a time limit on the question. Your relationship with Terence could last sixty years, and the Tarot can't extrapolate that far into the future, nor include all the ups and downs and twists that may arise between you. Technology stocks will doubtless rise and fall over time; what period are you looking at? Make the time period reasonably short, because Tarot is most accurate over short periods; over time, more and more variables creep in. So a reasonable question might be, "What are the energies surrounding a relationship between me and Terence over the coming year?"

Spreads and Techniques

You can, of course, use the standard Gestalt Tarot spread described earlier, or the condensed spread. You can choose any of the other spreads described in this book and use the Gestalt technique with them. Any of them will work for a solitary reader.

Many people prefer a simpler technique for day-to-day guidance: choosing one card the first thing in the morning, and meditating on it. From it, you can learn how the energy of the day is shaping up, and what situations to watch out for. Let's suppose you draw the Seven of Rods, which depicts a man holding a wooden staff, with other staves sticking up randomly in front of him. Now ask yourself the kind of questions you would ask the querent if you were reading for someone else.

What does the picture feel like to you? At some point in your life, that card might look like a man under attack by several mysterious and unseen assailants. Another day it might look like someone industriously building a home. Let's say that today it just looks confused and chaotic. You notice that the staves seem to be unaligned, of different lengths, with no pattern or order. You suspect that today's schedule is going to look like that—lots of energy and no organization or progress.

So you've gotten a glimpse of the day that lies before you. What you do about this information is up to you. Perhaps you will think about your priorities, choose a single, important goal, and vow that you will not be distracted by anything else until it is achieved. Maybe you will lock your office door and let the answering machine handle your telephone calls. To simplify your day, you might reschedule some meetings that have nothing to do with your most crucial projects.

You could check your astrological calendar and see if you're coming up on a Mercury retrograde, Moon void-of-course, or other astrological event that would affect the Tarot card's message. ("Mercury retrograde" refers to a period when the planet Mercury *appears* to reverse the direction of its orbit, because of its position relative to the Earth. Most astrologers believe that communication tends to break down during this time, until Mercury goes direct again. A "Moon void-of-course" refers to the period when the Moon has made its last conjunction within a given constellation, but has not yet entered the next constellation in its apparent path. Many astrologers suggest that any project launched during this window of time is likely to falter or fail.)

If you believe that the color of your clothing affects your day, you might decide to wear something that connotes calmness and order, such as a royal blue, or discipline and structure, such as black. Perhaps you would choose to wear a talisman to counteract the confusion, or pause to do some mental focusing exercises during the day. You might decide not to fight the energies, and instead take the day off and work in your garden.

If asking yourself open-ended questions doesn't lead you to new insights, try simply becoming the figure in the card. Stand or sit in the same posture as the main figure, imagine that you are clothed as he or she is, and holding whatever objects the figure has. Then close your eyes and visualize the card's environment around you: sea shore, mountains, whatever the card shows. Ask yourself what kind of person that individual is, and how they might feel in the situation depicted by the card. When you feel that you have made an empathetic connection with the figure, then focus your thoughts on your original question. If there is more than one figure in the card, try becoming each in turn. You should be able to view the situation from a new perspective, and find the answer you seek.

Pitfalls

The most obvious difficulty with reading for yourself is that you are biased in any question that affects you directly. When reading for a stranger, it is relatively easy to stay objective in your questions and avoid interpreting for them. It becomes harder to stay neutral when reading for a friend or family member because you know and care about the querent. Reading for yourself, you have to first illuminate your fears and desires, and then get past them to touch your intuitive sense of the truth that underlies your emotions.

Suppose you are reading for yourself and you turn up the Death card. Perhaps your first, gut-level reaction is panic: "Am I going to die? I don't want to die!" Then you must acknowledge your fear of death, set it aside, and ask what else the card might mean. After further study you decide that the card refers to transformation, and that you are actually the figure on the horse—the agent of change. You realize that your workplace is really dysfunctional, and that you are in a position to make some key changes that will improve things for everyone. It's obvious that some of your coworkers will fear any change, and fear you if you make it happen—just as most people fear the image of death in the card. You decide to "ride forth on your white horse" and launch the changes anyway. Had you stopped with your first reaction—fear, even panic—you would not have gotten to the real meaning of the card ("real" in the sense of useful).

We can distort the potential usefulness of a reading out of fear, but also out of desire—because we want a certain outcome very badly. Be clear up front what you want the Tarot to show you, admit it out loud, then go on to look at the cards for interpretations that might not match your fantasies. As an example, suppose you want to know if you and your boyfriend Jethro can have a stable and loving relationship. You draw the Knight of Swords: a grim warrior stares ahead, and flames from a burning tower reflect redly from his sword. Your first reaction might be: "He's protecting me—he must love me if he's willing to fight for me!"

But you know that's exactly what you *want* to believe. So you set that thought aside, and look more closely for alternative meanings. After a minute you realize that the warrior is not obviously protecting anyone; in fact, there's no one else in the picture. He just looks grim and focused, not protective. You remember that Jethro is extremely focused on his career, and tends to regard coworkers as rivals—even enemies. Everything takes second place—a distant second place—to his job. Often when he is with you he will talk about his work in very aggressive terms, and almost seem to forget you are there.

The card is indeed an accurate portrait of Jethro—but as he really is, not as you wish he were. Had you stopped with the first, easy interpretation—the one you wanted to be true—you might have made a serious mistake. By forging on past your desire, you found the truth; an unpalatable truth, but still more useful than a romantic fantasy.

Acting from fear or desire, we may give in to the temptation to change the result by choosing "just one more card" . . . and another . . . and another. You may do this because you don't like what you're seeing in the cards. It is much like the person who tosses a coin to decide something, doesn't like the way the coin lands, and then quickly says, "Best two out of three!" . . . "Best three out of five!" . . . and so on. If you keep drawing cards, eventually you'll get one you like; but you won't get much insight into the problem, and you will be uncomfortably aware that you manipulated the result and that your final good card doesn't mean a thing.

You might also keep adding cards because you want a more definite answer than the Tarot can provide at the time. The future is not carved in stone, and anything we predict can be altered by people acting with free will—including you. We may not find a clear answer in the Tarot because there are too many variables involved: some of the key players haven't made important decisions, or the outcome of a situation depends on whether you burn your breakfast and go to work in a bad mood, or eat at the Waffle House and show up with a happy tummy.

Adding one or two or three cards *may* provide clarification. Adding more than that may just get you more and more confused, until there are seventy-eight cards on the table and you have absolutely no idea what the answer is to your original question. Rather than adding more cards, it's often wise to more thoroughly explore the ones you already picked; the answer may already be in front of you.

The last pitfall has already been implied: the temptation to believe that the future revealed in a Tarot reading is immutable, kismet, karma, destiny, fate—in short, you're stuck with it. Always remember that the Tarot can reveal trends or extrapolations, but never a guaranteed future. Believing we have no control over our lives can be a self-fulfilling prophecy; but believing we can change things is also self-fulfilling. If you don't like what you see ahead of you, don't walk hopelessly into it—change your direction. If necessary, imagine the future you want, do another reading, and ask, "How can I change things so that this, the future I choose, comes to pass?"

Tarot cards are like your car's headlights—they can help you see what's on the road ahead, but you're the one holding the steering wheel.

Checking Your "Inner Bell"

You have within you what Marion Weinstein, author of *Positive Magic* (Phoenix Pub., 1985), has called an "inner bell." This is your deep awareness of what is right and true. When it gives you a message about your own actions, you could call it your conscience or moral compass; it's that instinct that warns you when a potential action would be wrong or harmful.

When it refers to an idea, opinion, or proposal, it might be called a "blarney detector." In Irish folklore, "kissing the Blarney Stone" (the rock set on the outside of a tower at Castle Blarney) is supposed to give one the "gift of gab," the ability to spin tales that are eloquent, convincing, and often pure nonsense.

Your inner bell or blarney detector is your ability to sense when a communication is misleading or untrue, no matter how plausible or desirable it seems on the surface. We all have this talent, but we don't always use it. Children will often ignore their inner bells because their appetites yell louder than their intuition; so a child at his birthday party may *know* that it's not smart to eat six pieces of cake, but it tastes so good.

Unfortunately, these same traits often carry over into adulthood. Have you ever talked yourself into doing something stupid despite that little voice inside telling you it was a mistake—and then mentally kicked yourself later because you should have known better? Well, most of us have.

But you don't have to ignore that inner signal. If your Tarot practice includes grounding and centering, and you enter that quiet place deep inside, that's where you can hear the inner bell most clearly. Ceremonial magicians call it "Entering the Silence," and in that silence you will know at once whether a message rings clear and true, or strikes a discordant note.

In the end, reading Tarot for yourself means that you courageously look at what's before you, and recognize the truth when it comes to you. Maybe that's all that life is about.

Enlisting Help

One of the hallmarks of wisdom is knowing your limitations—and when to yell for help. No one is completely self-sufficient, and no matter how centered and experienced you are, the time may come that you simply cannot do a clear reading for yourself. There is no shame in that. It just means that it's time to admit that you're not a superhero, and ask a friend, teacher, spiritual leader, or professional reader to lend their skills.

Surprisingly, the moment you become the querent instead of the reader, your inner bell may snap back on and help you recognize the answers you need. Maybe it's because the pressure is off and you are not facing the issue alone; maybe it's because you start looking at your life more objectively, through the reader's eyes. Whatever the reason, you will be on the road toward self-understanding again, and you will have given another person the gift of being able to help you find your path. So read for yourself when you can, and let another help when you can't. It's that simple.

Chapter 8

The Gestalt Reading

Gestalt Tarot is not a tool for the lazy mind. It usually offers no simple answers or fairy-tale endings. It places responsibility for a person's life squarely in their own lap. It is not a plaything offering a pleasant escape from reality, but a window deep into that reality: the reality in each human mind and heart.

The reading begins long before the two of you sit down at the table together. It really begins when you agree to do the reading.

A Clear Contract

As soon as you are requested to do a reading, you need to clarify several things with the client:

1. Do you charge for the reading? (See Chapter 11, "The Professional Reader.")

2. What day and date are convenient for both of you? Always discuss both; some clients will remember "Thursday" where they might forget "May 17th."

3. What time will the reading begin and how long will it take?

4. Where will the reading take place? If the client is to come to your home or shop, what are the directions? Remind them to call you if they become lost en route. If you are going to visit their home, do you understand the directions?

5. Does the client need to bring anything? You may ask them to bring their favorite Tarot deck, if that will make them more comfortable doing the reading; or a relaxing tape or CD they like. You may have little traditions or rituals special to your style, such as asking them to bring incense or a flower as a thank-you for whatever deities you ask for guidance.

Creating the Environment

It is more important that the environment work for the querent than for you. For them, a Tarot reading may be challenging and unfamiliar, while you should be skilled and experienced enough to function even if the music or lighting is not exactly what you would like.

A simple, uncluttered décor is ideal. A vase of flowers, a nice painting or two, or a couple of art objects would be fine; but too many magical or New Age knick-knacks will only distract from the reading. A soft, fairly neutral color on the walls and carpet will help the client relax and focus.

The room should be clean and fresh-smelling; some find it difficult to concentrate when there are unpleasant odors in the air, unidentifiable items strewn everywhere, or cockroaches the size of raccoons scurrying under the couch. Don't rely on the romance of low lighting to obscure last week's pizza crusts or drunken strangers left over from Saturday's party.

Many readers prefer candlelight, since this encourages imagination and intuition; however, Gestalt Tarot requires fairly good lighting, since the querent will be examining each card closely. Since your clients' eyesight will vary, you will need to be able to adjust the lighting, either by adding candles, using a dimmer switch, or arranging two or three lamps until the querent is happy.

You may wish to have soft music playing to set a meditative mood. Some readers like to have fresh flowers nearby, and a light incense burning; have it ready, but do not light it until you are sure it is acceptable to the querent; they may have asthma or allergies. A side table with coffee or other refreshments adds a nice touch.

Try to find a balance between a mysterious, enchanting ambiance where the client can set free their imagination and see with starlight vision—and an environment so ordinary and mundane that the client feels faintly silly taking the Tarot seriously. If in doubt, go very light on the special effects; much better to have a sparse, spare decor than to go overboard with mystical gewgaws. Plastic skulls and dripping black candles can only damage your credibility.

Reader and querent should be seated at the same height, whether in chairs on the opposite sides of a small table, or cross-legged on the floor if the querent is limber enough. You will be working for at least half an hour, occasionally up to two hours; so when in doubt, sit at a table. The tradition for Gestalt Tarot is that the querent sits in the north, the seat of power and direction of wisdom, since it is their wisdom that will be tapped rather than your own. The diagram cloth or board should be between you, facing the querent. If you will be tape-recording the session, or taking notes, have your equipment ready and waiting. I discourage querents from taking their own notes, because it distracts too much from their concentration on the cards. Better for the reader to take the notes, and share them with the querent at the end.

Before the client arrives, take a few moments to relax and perhaps meditate, to leave the rest of the world behind and prepare to enter the querent's world.

When the Querent Arrives

Welcome them, let them settle at the table and become comfortable with the surroundings, making small talk to help them to relax. Offer them a drink, perhaps water, fruit juice, or tea. If you want incense, mention the type you have in mind and ask how they would feel about it: "Sometimes people like to have a little incense going; I have cedar and sandalwood. Do you like either of those fragrances, or no incense at all?" Ask them if they like the music, or would prefer silence.

Helping the Querent Relax

Some readers may have heard of Rhine cards, which are used in experiments to explore psychic skills such as telepathy. There are five simple designs in a Rhine deck, such as a star, a square, or three wavy lines. The subject of the test must try to tell what design is on a given card without seeing it, either by touching the back of the card, or looking at the back, or *seeing* it through the eyes of another person when the tester looks at the design.

Tests of psychic phenomena show that people are most likely to be accurate on Rhine card experiments when they feel relaxed and confident. The same is true in working with Gestalt Tarot. Querents who are tense, nervous, and uptight are less likely to discover useful insights.

A tense person is halfway to the fight-or-flight reaction of our earliest ancestors when they encountered a dangerous or unfamiliar situation. Tarot involves neither; clubbing something over the head (especially the reader) or running away into the jungle are not helpful in getting an accurate reading.

Unfortunately not all querents are skilled in dealing with stress or using conscious relaxation techniques. As the reader, you can help by observing whether the querent is tense, drawing their attention to their mental and emotional state, and suggesting some simple methods of relaxation. These might include stretching, breathing slowly (with an emphasis on the exhalation), thinking about a comfortable and familiar place the querent knows, or chatting about the weather or the family dog.

The reader's attitude can help a great deal. If you are relaxed, confident, and charming, your mood will set an example. In effect you become the role model for "How One Behaves During a Tarot Reading." Once the querent is settled, introduce them to Gestalt Tarot.

Explaining Gestalt Tarot

With Gestalt Tarot, the querent is not an idle spectator whose only functions are to listen and remember. With Gestalt, the querent does at least half of the work, which is as it should be; the reading is about the querent's life, not the reader's.

The querent must understand how Gestalt Tarot works. Of course it is up to the reader to explain it clearly, but then it becomes the querent's responsibility to ask questions until they are sure of the process. Some clients will have had readings before (though probably not Gestalt readings), while others may be completely new to Tarot. In either case it's a good idea to have a little introductory explanation ready.

For a querent who is new to Tarot, you might say something like this: "Have you ever had any experience with Tarot before? No? Well, it's a form of divination; that is, a way to get information or insights that we might otherwise never know. There's nothing supernatural about it, no ghosts or spirits manipulating the cards. Nevertheless, it can be pretty impressive. One thing you need to understand: Tarot won't tell you what *must* happen in the future, or what you *should* do. You always have free will; you are always responsible for making your own choices. Tarot can show you what the pattern of your life is now, and what might happen if you continue on the same path. It can tell you in general what might happen if you make other choices. But you make the decisions. Tarot just gives you more information to help you decide.

"We'll be using a method called Gestalt Tarot, where you'll pick the cards and I'll ask you lots of questions about what you see in them. You won't be sitting there passively while I tell you all about your life; you'll be participating actively in the process. The meanings of the cards won't come out of a book, but out of your own life and experiences. I believe this is a lot more powerful and effective than some of the other ways Tarot can be read.

"Do you have any questions before we begin? Okay then, here's the deck. Why don't you take a moment and just look through the cards before we get started."

For a querent who has had Tarot readings before, you might say something like this: "This may be different from the readings you've had before. We'll be using a method called Gestalt Tarot . . . " and so on.

Clarifying the Question or Issue

A reading will often give the best results if the question posed, or issue discussed, is very clear. You will need to ask the querent what question they would like to consider, and help them frame it in a way that a Gestalt Tarot spread can respond to.

Remember, this form of Tarot does not provide a "Yes-No" answer. Here are some examples of questions that would be difficult to work with:

- "Should I take the job I've been offered with Pemrose Incorporated or stay where I am?"

- "Would I be happier if I married Ralph or Ishmael?"

- "Is it best if I finish my degree in marine psychology or join the Kirov Ballet?"

All of these involve value judgments that only the querent can make. The Tarot might help them realize their present job is more secure, but Pemrose would be more challenging; that life with Ralph would be emotionally rich, but marrying Ishmael would lead to travel and wealth; or that finishing their MP degree would bring a career filled with professional advancement, while dancing with the Kirov would be artistically fulfilling. But Tarot won't tell them what choice to make, and neither will a reader who respects their right to control their life.

It may make more sense to ask a less value-laden question, such as:

- "What are the energies surrounding a career at Pemrose? In my present company?"

- "If I marry Ralph, what will characterize the relationship? If I marry Ishmael?"

- What sort of career would result if I finish my degree and enter marine psychology? If I join the Kirov Ballet?"

Note that each of these requires two readings, unless you use the Comparison Spread outlined in chapter 10. However, the main point is that Tarot won't make a querent's decisions for them—only provide an extrapolation of paths, a glimpse of future probabilities.

Some clients don't have a specific question or issue, at least that they consciously recognize or are willing to admit. For these, you can offer to do a general life reading. This may cover broad issues in the individual's life, but more frequently a very specific concern will emerge during the reading, arising from the querent's subconscious and demanding to be addressed. It is almost as though the Tarot speaks aloud, saying, "You claim to have no particular questions or problems, but inside you know better, and we are going to deal with it right now."

If this kind of general reading quickly focuses in on a specific issue, you can discuss the situation candidly with the querent: "Look, I know you said you wanted a general reading, but the Tarot [i.e., the querent's subconscious mind] seems to believe you have a very specific concern in this area. Shall we explore it?"

Content-Free Readings

Occasionally you may encounter a client who desperately wants guidance but doesn't want to tell you what the problem is. Perhaps they are embarrassed, or don't trust your discretion, or promised another party that they would never tell a soul—something. Can you help them?

Yes. It is entirely possible to do a useful, in-depth reading on an issue without ever knowing what it is. In one sense it is more difficult for you, the reader, because you will have a more difficult time framing questions. Even worse, you may be consumed with curiosity. However, the good news is that you will be extremely objective: not knowing what the issue is, you can hardly have opinions about it.

Shuffling and Layout

One of the most obvious things the querent does is shuffle the cards, (meanwhile concentrating on the question or issue), lay out the deck in three parts, reassemble them, lay out a card on each space in the spread, and turn them over one at a time.

What's that all about? Couldn't you as reader do that just as well or even better, more quickly and efficiently? You will certainly be tempted to the first time a client with small hands struggles painfully with shuffling.

Some readers would like to believe that the querent handles the cards because somehow their fingers will select exactly the right card and put it in exactly the right place on the spread while being guided by spirits, astral entities, or guardian angels. Actually, this kind of intervention is not required for the reading to be useful. Whatever force is behind the selection and layout of the cards, it doesn't matter which cards arrive on the spread or what order they're in; a good reader will help the querent find sense in it.

So why does the querent need to handle the cards? First, because this involves them kinesthetically in the process. ("Kinesthetic" refers to the human senses other than sight and hearing. It includes touch, movement, smell, taste, and sensitivity to heat and cold, among other senses.)

Research has shown that we experience and remember things more vividly when we touch them, rather than just hearing or seeing them. The reading will stay in the client's memory longer and more clearly if they touch the cards (and, by the way, if they smell incense, sip coffee, and shake your hand).

Second, handling the cards makes the client feels more empowered. The cards they interpret are the ones *they* chose, the ones *they* put in those places. Never mind that the placement of particular cards is irrelevant; this is a symbolic gesture, a lead-in to the part of the reading where their involvement is not only relevant but crucial. It begins to prepare them for the idea that it's their reading, not yours; that they will find the meaning in the cards, apply it to their lives, and make their own life choices based on what they've learned.

Once the question is formulated, have the querent shuffle the deck while they are thinking about the question, and when they feel ready, divide the deck into three parts, and lay them next to each other on the table or floor. Explain that the querent will know which pile should be on top when the deck is reassembled; perhaps one pile will seem to stand out visually. More kinesthetically oriented querents may pass their hands over each pile; one will *feel* different. A few, very auditory querents might need to imagine a steady hum as they pass a hand over the piles; the pitch or loudness will change with one of them. When they discover the pile that is different, they put the stacks back together with that one on top.

Now ask the querent to take one card at a time—from the top or from inside the deck—and place it face-down on a position in the spread diagram. Explain that the card will seem *drawn* to one particular spot; if they are not sure which spot is *right*, they can use the visual, auditory, or kinesthetic techniques described in the last step. (You might think that many people, especially those who do not normally use psychic techniques, would have difficulty with this step. In fact most querents adapt easily.)

If you are taking notes, note which position was covered first, second, etc. Because the querent can see the positions while laying down the cards, this can be a clue to what they consciously think are the most important issues—especially if they have had a Gestalt reading previously and are familiar with the meanings of each position on the spread.

When all the spaces on the spread are covered by cards, ask the querent to choose any card and turn it face-up. If the card is inverted from the querent's viewpoint, then rotate it: *all cards are read right-side up* in Gestalt Tarot. There are no reversed meanings because the querent is discovering their own, personal, unique interpretation, and that would be difficult to do if they had to examine the card upside-down. Take note, also, of what order the querent turns over the cards. This can be an indication of what issues their subconscious believes are the most important issues.

A Word About Focus

Whether the querent's issue is as broad as "My Life" or as specific as "Should I Marry George," it is important that they stay focused during the reading. Before and after the actual reading, they can chit-chat as much as they wish about politics, Tarot in general, or how their Aunt Martha used to read tea leaves for the Methodist minister. Once the reading begins, watch for the querent who still wants to talk about anything else but the subject at hand.

Wandering attention, clever diversions, and outright escapism are not unknown during Tarot readings. Many people just don't like to think about their life challenges and choices; it's much easier to watch somebody else's problems on TV, knowing they will solve everything and find happiness in forty minutes, not counting commercials.

Not only is it hard for some querents to think about their troubles, but talking about them in front of a stranger is even worse. What if this wise and perceptive Tarot reader (you) thinks they are stupid for being in their situation, or stupid for not knowing what to do, or just thinks they are wearing stupid shoes? The querent may be very self-conscious about revealing their problems, and worried about what you might think.

If the querent is coping with a problem or a difficult decision, you can help by reassuring them that many people have the same kinds of problems, and that it is possible to understand the issues and make good choices. Help them imagine how good it will feel when they have faced the situation, dealt with it, and moved on. When they slide away from the subject, gently refocus as often as required.

Suspension of Logic and Analysis: Listening to the Heart

In the end, few of our insights, understandings, or choices in our personal lives rest on logical analysis. If you are an astronomer or a budget analyst, cold logic is highly useful in your profession. If you are a full-time homemaker, it is logical to start cooking the meatloaf before you pick up the kids from soccer or ballet lessons, so dinner can be ready on time.

For the big questions, our hearts rule. Whom to marry. Which house to buy. Whether to have children. Even what field of work to enter. Many of us could have entered more lucrative professions. When we hear about the income someone else makes, we might think to ourselves, "Why didn't I go into that field? I could have made a fortune and retired by now!" Financially, we might think we made some illogical choices. But if we followed our hearts, and are doing the work we love, then those were really the only choices that could have worked.

When a client is in the middle of a reading, *and begins to speak reason at the expense of their feelings*, the reader can help them consider the emotional side of the question as well. Ultimately Tarot is most useful when it allows us to read our own hearts, because that is the source of our motivations and choices. If you use Tarot to help a client find the most sensible, logical, reasonable, rational decision—then chances are they'll either follow it and be miserable or ignore it and do what they feel like doing. In either case, what was the reading for?

Opening Channels to Younger Self

Much of the value of Gestalt Tarot is that it elicits information from the querent's subconscious, sometimes called the Deep Mind, Younger Self, or Inner Child. This is the part of the human mind that stores memory and generates our emotional lives. It is the home of our passions, our loves and hates, our subjective feelings and intuition, of art and imagination.

Many people try to live only in their conscious minds, because they are afraid of this other part: what Freud called the *id*. The popular conception of the id or subconscious is that it is crawling with dark desires, unnatural lusts, hidden fears, and perversity of all kinds.

By contrast, the conscious or rational mind seems so civilized, orderly, and safe. Science fiction buffs may want to contrast the clean, high-minded, logical world of *Star Trek*, where most problems can be solved by computer analysis or a nice clean laser shot, and the world of the *Alien* series, which is dark and out of control, and fraught with terror.

The subconscious is the seat of physical sensation, emotion, and memory. However messy or frightening such things are to some, that is where we live a great part of our lives. Some would go further, saying that it is the subconscious that governs our lives. A Tarot reading that ignores these areas and works only in the sphere of ideas and logic is skewed to the point of uselessness.

Encourage your clients to think of the subconscious not as Freud's disreputable id, but rather as Younger Self. Sure, there are some intense feelings and bad memories there, but it is also the home of playfulness, imagination, and delight. In many ways our Younger Selves are like children or pets; they can be wayward and messy, but when approached with love and consistency, they are a joy.

Your clients are going to need imagination to get through a Gestalt reading, and they are going to have to recognize their feelings, physical sensations, and key memories if they are to holistically understand the directions of their lives and make useful choices.

You encourage the querent by the questions you ask. Not, "What do you think about this card?" but, "How do you feel about this card?" or, "What does this figure want?" or, "What do you need?" Ask, "Does this figure remind you of anyone?" or "Can you imagine what the sensations would be, standing on the beach with a sword in your hand, feeling the wind blow through your hair?" Talk feelings and memories and sensations, and smells and tastes and wishes; use the language of myth and magic and fairy tales. Once Younger Self is involved, then you are doing Tarot with a whole person.

All this means that you are not simply a reader, but a counselor in the best sense of helping people explore themselves, the difficult parts as well as the easy ones. It is a large responsibility; but the alternative is to do "Tarot Light," where you amuse the client with pretty pictures, superficial platitudes, and feel-good predictions, then send them home. Now that's entertainment—but it's hardly Tarot at its best.

Being Honest, Facing the Truth

Sometimes things come out in a Gestalt reading that the querent would rather not know. He is angry at his father and doesn't want to admit it. She made a self-destructive choice in her husband but is terrified to face the idea of divorce and life on her own. He has invested six years in college and four years after that in a profession that gives him no joy. The list goes on.

During a Tarot reading, unexpected and difficult truths may emerge. Part of your job is to guide the reading—not to your truth, but to the client's. You can ask the tough questions, but you cannot make a querent see the truth. Occasionally a client will stand before a truth that is utterly crystal clear to you—and be oblivious. Some emotional or mental block makes it invisible to them. Your temptation will be to offer advice: "Your relationship clearly isn't working—you should give it up," or "Can't you see, it's what you've wanted to do all your life—go for it!"

Do not give advice. The whole point of Gestalt Tarot is to help the querent discover what they need to know, not to hand it to them on a plate. If you try to gift them with a truth that seems obvious to you, they will at the least be disempowered: it is your answer, not theirs, and it is quite possible that they will resist the truth when it comes from you. If a person makes an omelet and it doesn't turn out well, often they'll eat it anyway; it's not very tasty, but it's theirs. It's just as true with an unpalatable insight. If you make a bad omelet and hand it to them (i.e., offer your hard truths or difficult advice), they may take a bite out of courtesy but they're not going to be happy with you; and at the first chance, they'll slip it under the table to the dog.

Encourage your clients to face their lives honestly and bravely. Then let them discover their own truths, in their own time.

Asking Open-Ended Questions

What all of this is leading up to is that the heart of Gestalt Tarot is asking the right kind of questions. They must be open-ended, not leading. Generally an open-ended question begins with "how," "why," or "what," and it cannot be answered with a simple "yes" or "no." Some sample questions that a reader might ask, along with responses from querents:

- "What is this person doing?" ("He's building something, maybe it's a wall or stockade . . ." etc.)

- "How does she feel about that?" ("She's mostly content, although there's a part of her that wishes . . ." etc.)

- "Why do you suppose he has come to this place?" ("I think he's searching for something . . ." etc.)

Non-open questions (leading questions) often begin with "is" or "does." Some examples:

- "Is this man a warrior?" ("Yes.")

- "Is the woman pleased about the situation?" ("No.")

- "Does he want to escape from that place?" ("Yes.")

The more open-ended your questions, the more the querent must reach into their imagination and emotions in order to answer. In doing so, they reveal themselves: they cannot guess at the motivations, feelings, and actions of the figures on the card without projecting themselves or their experience on to those figures.

At the simplest level, the querent may project themselves directly into every figure. At some level they are pondering, "What would I feel . . . or think . . . or do if that were me?" Occasionally they will see someone else in a card—someone important to them such as a parent, spouse, boss, or adversary. Exploring those figures can help the querent understand a great deal about their relationships with significant people in their lives.

Avoiding Leading Questions

It is extremely tempting to allow our feelings to slant the questions we ask, or lead us to assumptions about where the querent is heading with a certain line of responses. To be effective, a Gestalt Tarot reader must stay clear and objective, and never lead the querent to a conclusion just because it makes sense to the reader.

A few examples of leading and nonleading questions follow:

Leading: "Would you say that this person is angry?"

Open-Ended: "How do you suppose this person feels?"

Leading: "Is she unhappy about having to make that choice?"

Open-Ended: "How does she feel about that choice?"

Leading: "Does this represent love and romance to you?"

Open-Ended: "What does this card symbolize for you?"

Leading: "Isn't it possible that he is about to leave on a long journey?"

Open-Ended: "What do you think he's going to do next?"

When a leading question is asked, many people will either be influenced to answer in the indicated way, or will agree just to be—agreeable. A few will contradict the reader just to assert their independence or because they like to be contrary. None of these responses will be very valuable, since they are all reactions to the reader's suggestion rather than a true response from the querent's heart and mind.

A Potpourri of Good Questions

Very often it is useful to begin with an extremely open, general question:

- "How do you feel about that card?"
- "What do you notice in this picture?"

If there is a single or central figure, you can ask about that individual:

- "What's this person doing?"
- "What kind of person do we have here?"
- "What do you suppose this person is feeling at this moment?"
- "What might have caused them to feel that way?"
- "What does this person want to happen next?"
- "If this person is looking at something beyond the edge of the frame, what is it?"
- "Where did this person just come from, and what were they doing there?"
- "How do you suppose he feels about that?"
- "What is this person going to do next?"
- "Why would he do that?"
- "Does this person face a choice or decision right now? What's keeping him from making a choice?"
- "What are his or her two main options?"
- "Is there a third choice that they haven't yet thought of?"
- "Is there a fourth option? A fifth?"
- "What kind of information would make this decision easier?"
- "How will they choose which is the best course of action?"
- "What choice do you think he or she will make?"
- "What kinds of drawbacks are there to that choice? Any more drawbacks?"
- "What will be the likely outcome of that decision?"

- "How will they feel about that decision a month from now? A year from now?"

- "If this person were to look at you and say something right now, what would they say?"

If there is more than one figure shown, you can ask the querent to explore their relationship:

- "How do these two feel about each other?"

- "What is their relationship?"

- "Why did they originally come together?"

- "How long have they known each other / been together?"

- "What do they do for each other that's positive?"

- "Do they have any negative impact on each other? In what way?"

- "What is this one's greatest contribution to the relationship?"

- "What does this one do that gets in the way of a healthy relationship?"

- "What will happen if they stay together for a long time?"

- "Is there one thing that they could do to make the relationship work better? Anything else?"

- "How does this third person affect their interaction?"

- "What do they need to do next?"

In all these questions, you are really asking the querent to consider their own situation or choices; but because they are projecting the situation on to a third party—the figure in the card—they can view it more objectively. In effect, you are asking the querent to step outside their frame of reference and see it from a more dispassionate perspective.

Of course, the querent may not project exactly their own situation on to the card figure; that would make it very difficult to maintain any objectivity. Instead, they may project an allegory, metaphor, or parallel situation. An example:

Reader: (Pointing to the Five of Swords, in which a smiling figure holds three swords while two discouraged-looking people wander away along a beach) "What's happening here?"

Querent: "Well, it looks like there's been a swordfight, and this smirking guy in the front won."

Reader: "How are the other people feeling about that?"

Querent: "What do you mean? Obviously they're not very happy about losing!"

Reader: "Well, was it an important battle, or just a friendly contest? How do they feel about it—philosophical, resigned, really upset?"

Querent: "Maybe it wasn't life-or-death . . . but I think they've lost to this dude before, like a lot of times. Like every time they fight. And he wins every time, and gathers up the swords, just smirking away—God, I hate that guy!"

[NOTE: It's not too likely that the querent really hates "that guy" as a nameless drawing on a card; "that guy" reminds him of someone.]

Reader: "Who does he remind you of?"

Querent: "No one . . . no, wait! It's my brother! All the time we were growing up, he was always the best at everything—sports, grades, music, you name it. And he smirked like that every time he beat us in a game or anything . . ."

Here the swordfight on the card became a metaphor for the competition between the querent and his brother. Because the figures had swords and medieval clothing, and thus superficially did not resemble the querent's family, he was able to keep the card's meaning at arm's length on a conscious level (though his subconscious certainly had made the connection), until his feelings became fully clear. Only then did the reader bring it home, allowing the querent to see past the props and costumes to discover the meaning for his own life.

Transition to Personal Meaning

As indicated above, querents will usually talk very freely about some stranger depicted in a card. It's all fantasy anyway, right? That's not a real person, is it? So it's safe to rattle on at length about his imaginary feelings, imaginary thoughts, and imaginary actions.

At some point you must gently guide the querent to the realization that the stranger in the card *is* the querent, or someone important to the querent, or both. Some clients show very little surprise when this becomes clear, others experience a sort of epiphany: "Oh. *Oh!* That's exactly how I feel about my husband!" Oddly enough, you can usually play this little game over and over with each succeeding card: "What does the figure in the card think? And what do you think? Surprise (for the ninth time)! You were describing your own thoughts all along!"

A few querents will get very cagey after the first time, and either refuse to play the game or put on a little smirk which seems to say, "Okay, I know it's really me in that card, but I'll pretend it's some mythical figure." For those who can't or won't project themselves into the cards, it is best to be very direct and move quickly from, "What feeling does this card seem to express?" to, "Does this echo your own feelings about your question in any way?"

Who Are Those People in the Cards?

Whenever possible, the reader should guide the querent to explore the figure in some depth before attempting to discover who it represents. An early revelation of identity may block all kinds of useful information from surfacing, because the querent may immediately switch to a "party-line" appraisal of the individual, repeating what they are "supposed" to feel about that person.

For example, let's look at two different ways a reading might go:

The Figure's Identity Revealed Early

Querent: "All right, I'll turn this one over . . . it's the Queen of Swords."

Reader: "Is there anyone in your life that reminds you of?"

Querent: "Uh . . . my mother, I guess."

Reader: "And what was your relationship with your mother like?"

Querent: "It was OK. We had our differences, but we loved each other."

The Figure's Identity Revealed Later

Querent: "All right, I'll turn this one over . . . it's the Queen of Swords."

Reader: "What kind of person is this? Can you tell me anything about her personality, her character?"

Querent: "I would say very hard, very demanding. High standards, intellectually sharp but critical and hard to get along with."

Reader: "So how would people close to her feel?"

Querent: "They would feel like they could never live up to her standards. Inadequate. Small."

Reader: "Does she remind you of anyone in your life?"

Querent: "Uh . . . wow. My mother. I still can hear her voice, very sharp and critical . . ."

In the first example, the Queen of Swords was connected with the querent's mother right away. The querent was immediately on guard, not wanting to look at the negative side of their relationship. Whether because of guilt ("I must have been a bad daughter") or social convention ("Daughters are supposed to love and respect their mothers"), the querent glossed over a situation that probably still affected her life. In the second example, some real issues were uncovered before the Queen was identified as the querent's mother. This might lead to an honest appraisal of their relationship and its continuing influence on the querent.

Reflective Listening

Often the reader can do the most good just by reflecting the querent's responses back to them, either word-for-word or paraphrased. This compels the querent to really listen to what they have just said, and may lead them to consider their feelings in more depth. Here is one example:

Reader: "You've said that he is a warrior. How does he feel about that?"

Querent: "About being a warrior? I think he's sick and tired of it. I think he wants to stop fighting and be at peace."

Reader: "He wants to stop fighting?" [Reflecting word-for-word.]

Querent: "Yeah. It seems like he's fought a million people, and there's no end in sight. His luck can't hold forever; he'd love to get out while he's still alive."

Reader: "So he's lucky he's survived this long, but he's got this feeling he's really at risk, that he's doomed unless he changes his life." [Paraphrase]

Reflective listening is an exception to the no-leading-questions rule. A reflected question or paraphrase, by its nature, asks for an elaboration, not a simple "yes" or "no."

Role~Playing the Cards

Actions speak louder than words. If the querent has trouble "getting into the head" of the figures in the cards and imagining their thoughts and feelings, acting out a figure may help the process. Even if the querent has a good imagination, getting them physically involved may help make the message more vivid.

This can be done simply by asking the querent to adopt the same pose or position as the figure in the card, and to imagine that they are dressed the same. However, if you are going to do a lot of Gestalt Tarot then you might enjoy collecting some simple props and costume items. If you have a staff, a heavy chalice, a pentacle, and a sword in your home to represent the Minor Arcana suits, then excellent. If not, make do with a broomstick, a wine glass, a tray, and a carving knife. You will need a "throne" (any chair), and some costumery (miscellaneous hats, scarves, capes, or fabric yardage).

The props and clothing do not have to be terribly authentic, since the querent won't be seeing themselves dressed up; simply feeling the items will help. You can get a lot of colorful costume pieces from thrift shops and yard sales, and can even purchase a new sword (decorative, not functional) for less than $100 from a mail-order catalog, or off the Internet.

So, at whatever time the querent gets stuck, or whenever they have made an intellectual discovery that you want to reinforce kinesthetically, invite them to "become the figure in the card" for a moment, with or without props and costume. They may close their eyes if that helps. Verbally help them into the role; for example:

"Now, you sit on the throne. You wear the Rose Crown, and are surrounded by great red blossoms; they signify passion and courage (the querent told you this earlier). In your left hand you hold a sword, gleaming bright and razor sharp. Feel its weight. Feel the authority and power that are yours alone. You *are* the Queen of Swords. Speak to me now, tell me what you feel."

This kind of experience can make the message of the Tarot infinitely more vivid and memorable. Do not use it for every card, but certainly for the most important ones.

Relating the Card to Its Position in the Spread

You may be surprised how much meaning a single card can contain, but stand by; it gets deeper. The personal symbolism of each card must be interpreted in the context of its position in the spread.

Thus the Page of Cups in the Mars position may have a very different meaning from the Page of Cups in the Saturn position. Let's compare these two examples:

Page of Cups in Mars

Reader: "So this young man, the Page of Cups, is talking to the fish in the cup? Why?"

Querent: "Yes . . . but what I mean is that he's talking to part of himself. The fish is his imaginary friend who is always there for him. It sounds pretty odd, but lots of kids have imaginary friends and I think this guy is so lonely that he kept his into adulthood."

Reader: "And this card is in the Mars position, which suggests 'action' or 'the male principle.' What does that suggest to you?"

Querent: "Action . . . there's something he should be doing? Like in a very, I don't know—assertive way? I think his fish friend represents his emotions. He's always analyzing his own emotions, being really wrapped up in himself and never really taking action to accomplish anything. I think he needs to stop talking to the fish, set some goals, and do something. Get a life."

Page of Cups in Saturn

Querent: ". . . and I think this guy is so lonely that he kept his into adulthood."

Reader: "And this card is in the Saturn position, which suggests 'opposition,' 'teacher,' 'obstacles,' or 'limitation.' What does that suggest to you?"

Querent: "It's holding him back in some way. He's learned something from having this imaginary friend—maybe he's actually learned a lot about himself—but now it's just getting in his way."

Reader: "How would it get in his way?"

Querent: "Well, being so focused on this fish friend means he doesn't have any real social life. And you can only grow so much in isolation; part of growing up means learning to deal with people, have relationships. Maybe he should be out there in the world making friends for real, instead of relying on an imaginary fish."

These examples show that the placement of the Page of Cups can give it very different meanings: in the Mars position the querent sees it as meaning "Set goals and take action," while in the Saturn position, the querent sees the meaning as "Get out in the world, meet people, and have relationships." Of course it's not always so easy. It may require several questions and some real digging to find out how a given card relates to its planetary position in the spread. But the more you study the meanings of the positions in Chapter 5, the easier it will become to help the querent find the relationship.

The Bigger Picture

As each card is analyzed, be sure to relate the card not only to its place on the diagram, but to previous cards. You may need to help the querent by reminding them what they have come up with from earlier cards, encouraging them to look for connections, and paraphrasing their insights. Just make sure that you don't put words in their mouth or subtly urge them to see the same things you see.

If there are unanswered questions once all the cards have been revealed and discussed, then the querent may pose another question and choose another card from the Da'ath pack, the part of the deck that hasn't been used. Explore this card in the same way as the others. You can repeat this process once or twice more, but don't let it drag on, card after card after card. Three cards are usually sufficient to glean all the remaining information needed. The Tarot itself is inexhaustible, but there is only so much information you can elicit before your mind tires.

Summing Up

As the reading draws to a close, you may want to summarize all that's been discussed: the individuals who appeared, their role in the querent's life, what issues have been addressed, and what the likely outcomes of certain actions will be. Go over the patterns once again:

1. Abundance or scarcity of Major Arcana.

2. Abundance or scarcity of each of the suits: Swords, Wands, Cups, and Pentacles.

3. Abundance or scarcity of Court cards: Kings, Queens, Knights, and Pages.

4. Cards in the upper half of the spread (conscious thought?) vs. the lower half (subconscious desires?).

5. Storyline progression following the order of the cards as they were revealed.

6. Chronological progression in the same order, or moving from the querent's left to right.

7. Frequent appearance of certain colors, or symbols, or lone figures vs. groups, or themes of any kind.

It is not helpful to leave the querent with a confused hash of insights and impressions, which are likely to fade quickly. Help them find the patterns and themes of their life reflected in the patterns and themes of the Tarot spread.

In any case you may wish to give the client a printed copy of the spread at the end, on which they can mark which cards they placed in each position, along with any other notes they want to make.

At the End of the Reading

When all is complete and you have said your good-byes, it is time to ground, center, and rest. You may need a nap, or a snack, or a walk in the woods, or a period of quiet meditation, or some hatha yoga or tai chi, or twenty laps in the municipal pool, or a quick game of tennis. Any of these will help you to physically change gears and mentally disconnect from the querent.

Making Choices

Almost the last part of a querent's responsibility is to make decisions and choices for themselves based on what they have learned through the Tarot reading. Once again, you cannot assume this responsibility for them.

Frequently you won't even learn what their choices are. A client may come to you, debating whether to take the fun, low-paying job in Hawaii or the high-powered, highly paid executive job in New York. After a fascinating and revealing reading, he may thank you and disappear without ever telling you his decision.

So be it. It is bad manners to run after a client screaming, "But what are you going to do?" More to the point, it's none of your business.

You can help a client discover their alternatives. You can help them explore the consequences of various choices. You can even help them see what may happen if they fail to make a decision. And there your part ends; the rest is up to the client.

Acting in Accord

Occasionally, in the midst of a reading, clarity comes to a client like a sunbeam from heaven. The client (we can call her Gertrude) sees the truth and knows *exactly* what she needs to do next. She may vow to take positive action, thank you extravagantly, and go off to change her life.

And nothing happens. Back out in the real world, with bills to pay and expectations from her family and so on, the insights of the Tarot reading fade, courage wanes, and the next time you see Gertrude, her life has not changed one iota.

Worse, she comes back next month and asks for another reading, which reveals the same truths, and leads to no more change than the first one. Gertrude is a fantasy junkie, who comes back again and again to catch glimpses of what her life could be, but will never take action to make it real.

At a reading a client may ask you for permission, approval, encouragement, or direction in what to do. "Oh, the cards say Fred is a tightwad but very affectionate; do you think I should marry him?" If you reply with either "yes" or "no," then you are opening the door to trouble. If your advice is wrong, you get blamed for the outcome. If your advice works out well, then the querent begins to become dependent on you for her important life decisions.

If you reply with several focused questions (such as, "Which is more important to you in a relationship, generosity or affection?" or "Do you suppose there's a man out there who is both generous and affectionate?"), then there is hope for you as a Gestalt Tarot reader.

If a client becomes insistent ("Stop asking me questions, just tell me what you think!"), you are well within your rights to say: "I can't advise you on that. You are the only one who can make such an important decision about your future."

You can hope a client will take action, and act in accordance with what the reading has shown, but you can never make it happen. And that is as it should be.

Chapter 9

Sample Tarot Readings

Let's follow a reading from beginning to end. Jenny comes to you with a question about her business. A couple of years ago, she started a home-based business creating and selling herbal products: soaps, lotions, shampoos, and a few other products. She wholesales her creations to several stores in the area; however, the products are very labor-intensive to make, sales remain at a steady trickle, and the business is not growing.

Now she is considering launching a major campaign to make the business grow: taking out a small-business loan, buying some equipment, expanding her line of products, hiring some help, and promoting her products more aggressively. She has talked to some of the retailers who already carry her products, and is getting some encouragement from friends and family. However, she is wondering what the Tarot has to say.

Reader: "I would be happy to help you explore this question. Have you ever had a Tarot reading before?"

Jenny, as *Querent:* "Yeah, once or twice, and it's always intrigued me. And my friend Michele recommended you, and said your reading was very helpful, and different from ones she'd had before."

Reader: "Okay, let me explain a little about Tarot. The cards may have first appeared in fifteenth-century Italy, and over the centuries a lot of new decks have been designed. Some haven't changed a whole lot in five hundred years, and some have designs that are pretty wild. Here's the deck I use: it's called the *Morgan-Greer* deck, and I use it because I like the artwork and the colors. Why don't you look through the deck a little bit?"

Jenny: "You're right, these are pretty, But I don't quite understand how kings and knights apply to my business situation."

Reader: "The cards deal with universal themes and situations. Don't let the old-fashioned costumes fool you, there will be a connection to your question. As for the reading being 'different,' we'll be using a method called Gestalt Tarot, where you'll pick the cards and I'll ask you lots of questions about what you see in them. Unlike other readings you've had, you'll be participating a lot in the process. The meanings of the cards won't come out of a book or my psychic connections to other planes, but out of your own life and experiences. I believe this is much more powerful and effective than some of the other ways Tarot can be read."

Jenny: "Oh. Okay, that makes sense. What do I do now?"

Reader: "Think about your question as you shuffle the cards a few times. . . . Okay, now divide them into three stacks. Which stack wants to be on top when you put the deck back together?"

Jenny: "Which stack wants . . . I don't understand."

Reader: "Look at the three stacks. Does one draw your attention more than the others? Does one seem a little more vivid or seem to almost glow?"

Jenny: "No, not really."

Reader: "I'm guessing that you're a kinesthetic kind of person, hands-on, like to use your hands and touch things?"

Jenny: "Oh yeah. I like growing my herbs, weeding and harvesting, making things with my hands. . . ."

Reader: "Then pass your hand over the three stacks; you might feel a different sort of energy from one of them."

Jenny: "Oh . . . yeah, this one almost seems to make my hand buzz. Put it on top?"

Reader: "Right. Now take the cards one at a time and place them face-down on the spread diagram here. You can take them from the top of the deck

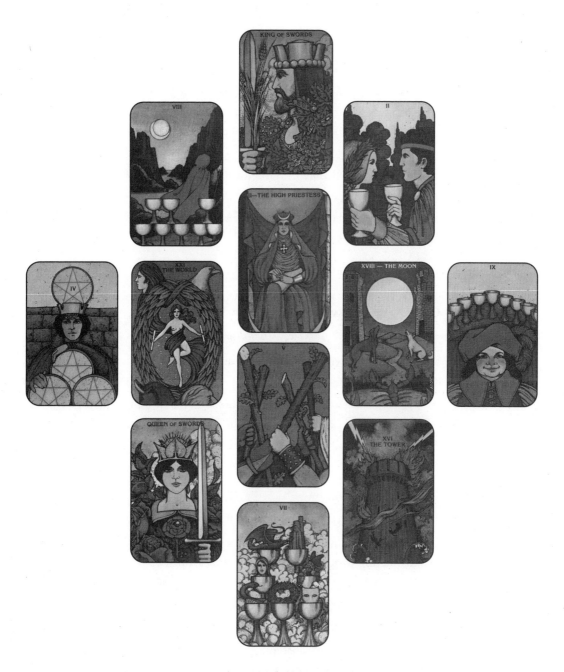

Sample Gestalt Tarot Reading

143

or from inside. Just put each card where it feels appropriate; don't think about it."

Jenny: "You mean it's like each card goes in a certain spot, and I'll know where to put it just by the feeling?"

Reader: "Yes. It might feel like each card is almost magnetically drawn to a certain place; or, if you pass the card over the spread, you may feel a vibration when it's over the right place."

Jenny: "Okay, I'll try." (She rapidly places cards in all twelve positions.) "Say, this part seems a little like mumbo-jumbo. Is all this really necessary?"

Reader: "No, but it helps you get focused and concentrate. Now you can turn over any one card. We'll explore that one and then turn over all the others one at a time."

Jenny: "All right." (She reaches up to the Sun position, and turns over the King of Swords.)

Card One: King of Swords in the Sun Position

Jenny: "Whoa, that's formidable. What does that mean?"

Reader: "That's what we're about to find out. You said this card is 'formidable.' Tell me about that."

Jenny: "I just meant that he—this king—looks very serious, very determined. He's not only a king, he has a big sword and he's willing to use it."

Reader: "Will he need to use it?"

Jenny: "Probably. I doubt he's carrying it just for fun."

Reader: "Does he have the skills to use it, if it becomes necessary?"

Jenny: "You know, I think he does. But he's not using it now; he's on his throne, making wise decisions and whatever kings do. The sword is a reminder that he will do whatever it takes to enforce his decisions."

Reader: "So how would you sum up the king's character and personality? What kind of man is he?"

Jenny: "He's very confident, absolutely certain of what he wants to do, and willing to fight for his beliefs. He's wise enough to think things through, to plan ahead, so he doesn't have to use the sword much, but it's there and he is absolutely willing to use it."

Reader: "Does that description remind you of anyone you know?"

Jenny: "Well—oh. Me, I guess. My friends say I have a one-track mind and can be pig-headed sometimes."

Reader: "This card is in the Sun position. That stands for the source of your power, what motivates you and keeps you going."

Jenny: "So, my personality is a source of power? My pig-headedness?"

Reader: "Well, yes, but I wouldn't call it that. How about calling it 'focus' and 'drive'? 'Pig-headedness' sounds like putting yourself down, and these qualities can be very valuable if they're combined with wisdom and foresight . . . as the king does. Tell me, do you find yourself using your sword often? Fighting for what you want?"

Jenny: "Driving on for what I want, yes. Not fighting with other people— at least very rarely. That isn't constructive. I think I know when to pull out the sword."

Reader: "Okay, let's go on. Turn over any other card."

Jenny: "How about this one?" (Turns over The World in the Venus space.)

Card Two: The World in the Venus Position

Reader: "What's happening here?"

Jenny: "There's a naked woman dancing in this big wreath. She's holding two wands. There are all kinds of animals and things around the edge, but she's not noticing them."

Reader: "So her attention is not on the figures surrounding her?"

Jenny: "Yeah . . . and that's kind of odd. I mean, there's a bull and a lion and a person and all, and she's oblivious, just staring straight ahead, and holding those wand things very carefully."

Reader: "Supposing she started noticing the animals and so on, what difference would that make? What if it were you?"

Jenny: "I would feel vulnerable, for one thing. She's practically naked. If I paid attention, I might at least see whether the people and animals were friendly or mean or just indifferent. At least I would know."

Reader: "Is there something in your business that you've been very focused on, and other things you have not been noticing?"

Jenny: (She is silent for a moment.) "Oh my god, I understand. The wands could represent my products. The person in the corner is a customer. I've been so focused on the products—the challenge and pleasure of making them—that I haven't paid much attention to the people who buy them!"

Reader: "So you've been concentrating on making the products and gotten out of touch with your customers?"

Jenny: "Yes. It's embarrassing to admit it, but yes. I've been thinking about expanding the line of products, and I've got some great ideas—what I think are great ideas—but I actually have no idea if they're what my customers want. If I go ahead without knowing more about my customers, I will be vulnerable like the woman in the card."

Reader: "Can you spell 'market survey?' (Jenny laughs.) What about the animals?"

Jenny: "Ummm. . . .They're my retailers, my competition, potential resources . . . pretty much everything outside my workroom, all the people and things I've been ignoring."

Reader: "Ready to do another card?"

Jenny turns over the Two of Cups, which is upside down.

Card Three: Two of Cups in the Uranus Position

Jenny: "Should I put it right-side up?"

Reader: "Yes. In Gestalt Tarot, all the cards are read right-side up. What's the first thing you notice?"

Jenny: "Well, it's very friendly, but there's these dark clouds or trees in the background, looming over the happy couple. It looks ominous."

Reader: "What could those dark clouds represent?"

Jenny: "The competition, maybe. Other companies that make products like mine, who might leap and gobble me up—well, gobble the market up—if I'm not careful."

Reader: "And the two people with the cups, who are they?"

Jenny: "They could represent me and my retailers. Everything seems fine right now, but there is this threat looming over us."

Reader: "This card is in the Uranus position, and refers to changes. Does that make any connection for you?"

Jenny: "Yes, it means that our working relationship may change, if I don't watch the competition and be ready with counteroffers if they try to take away my retailers."

Reader: "Turn over another card?"

Jenny turns over the Moon card right below the last one.

Card Four: The Moon in the Jupiter Position

Jenny: "I don't know what to make of this card."

Reader: "What's your first impression? How does it feel?"

Jenny: "Spooky, and confusing. Here's this little lobster that looks like it wants to leave the pond and travel along the path—why would a lobster do that?—but there are two dogs guarding the path. The moon is looking down on it all."

Reader: "Let's focus on one part at a time. You say the lobster wants to follow the path. What are some reasons why it might do that?"

Jenny: "You want me to explain what might motivate a lobster?"

Reader: "Sure, why not?"

Jenny: "Okay. Uh, maybe the pond is too small, or drying up. Maybe it wants to go look for a mate. Maybe there's been an oil spill and the pond is polluted. Maybe it's just a restless personality. Maybe it's suicidally depressed and wants to end it all, but the pond pharmacist won't give it any more sleeping pills."

Reader: "See, you can get into a lobster's head."

Jenny: "Such an achievement."

Reader: "Let's take the first possibility that came to you: '. . . the pond is too small, or drying up.' Can you relate that to your business?"

Jenny: "Wow, I actually can. I've been considering expanding my product line because the business feels—constricted. Like we're not growing or getting anywhere. The pond's too small. And sales have been off a little; I worried that I'm saturating the market locally—'the pond's drying up.'"

Reader: "Why hasn't the lobster actually left the pond, and gone off to explore new ponds?"

Jenny: "Because there are these big fierce dogs there, that might eat the lobster. Of course they're not even looking at the lobster, they're baying at the moon."

Reader: "What do the dogs represent, as far as your business goes?"

Jenny: "They're . . . well, they're the competition. The big herbal companies. They might 'eat up my business. . . .' No, that's silly, I'm in a very specialized niche, they wouldn't care what I did . . . I don't know. I don't know what the dogs symbolize."

Reader: "If you did know, what would they be?"

Jenny: "You know what? They're my fears. Fear of failure, fear of expanding, fear of more responsibility and competition. Even fear that I might succeed and have a much bigger, more successful company that I would be responsible for. I guess it's been a pretty comfy little pond. And yet—I do want more. Gee, am I a little conflicted about this or what?"

Reader: "This card is in the Jupiter position: 'Things in your favor, positive influences.' Any idea why?"

Jenny: "Because in spite of my fears, I'm restless and ready to take some risks, and I guess that must be a good thing. Can I pick another card?"

Reader: "Go for it."

Jenny turns over the Tower card.

Card Five: The Tower in the Saturn Position

Jenny: "Uh, oh. This can't be good."

Reader: "Why do you say that?"

Jenny: "Because lightning is striking the tower and it's on fire and people are falling out of it. It's not exactly 'The Rainbow Fairies Go on a Picnic,' is it?"

Reader: "Talk about the lightning."

Jenny: "It's sudden, it's powerful, it's a blinding flash, the tower is set on fire."

Reader: "Look at the tower. How do you feel about it?"

Jenny: "It looks like it was very strong, very stout. Safe. Well, it should have been. The people who lived there thought it was safe, anyway. Wrong!"

Reader: "How did it feel to live in that tower?"

Jenny: "It was probably pretty cozy. Maybe a little confining, with all that stone around you, and those tiny windows. I think it might feel safe, but it would be pretty claustrophobic after a while."

Reader: "It's in the Saturn position: 'Obstacles, things in your way.' Point to the obstacle on the card."

Jenny: (Starts to touch the lightning, then hesitates.) "Obviously the lightning—wait. Wait. Lightning's not an obstacle, it's pure energy. The tower's the obstacle!"

Reader: "The 'confining, claustrophobic' tower?"

Jenny: "Absolutely. The lightning is actually clearing it out of the way, or opening it to the sky. I have been confining my business to a few products in a few local stores; I built the stone tower around myself because I was afraid to expand."

Reader: "And the 'blinding flash,' the lightning, is . . . ?"

Jenny: "Revelation. Insight. Realizing that I've limited myself out of fear."

Reader: "Let's look at another card, if you're ready."

Jenny: "Let's go over here." (Turns over the Queen of Swords.)

Card Six: The Queen of Swords in the Mars Position

Jenny: "Oh, I like this one. She's very strong."

Reader: "What's the first thing you notice in the card?"

Jenny: "Her eyes. They're fearless and direct. She's not afraid to look at anything in front of her, no matter how scary it is. And she has a sword. She will use it if need be, just slash away anything that gets in her way."

Reader: "Jenny, I want you to try something. Would you come over here for a minute?" (The reader takes a fancy brocaded cloth from a shelf, and drapes it over a large chair.) "Please sit here."

Jenny: "What's this?"

Reader: "Your throne, Your Majesty." (The reader gets out a cloak, a crown made of gilded cardboard, and a real sword; then dresses Jenny in the cloak and crown.) "Here, hold the sword just like the figure in the card is holding it."

Jenny: "This is cool. What do I do?"

Reader: "I'll hold the card in front of you. Look at it. I want you to sit in the same position as this queen, and *become* her. Hold your sword like you mean it. You can feel your robes of state, feel the golden crown upon your head; roses surround you, yet you do not fear their thorns. You are strong, confident; your keen gray eyes see all that is before you. You *are* the Queen of Swords!"

Jenny: (Closing her eyes.) "I am the Queen of Swords."

Reader: "Before you, one of your subjects kneels. She has come to you for your wise counsel. She has a small business in herbal products, and desires to know whether she should expand it, what she should do."

Jenny: (After a moment of silence.) "I say to you, look at your venture with clear eyes. Be fearless. Prune what must be pruned, that your business may flourish as my roses do. Then move ahead steadily and courageously." (She opens her eyes.) "I like being the Queen of Swords."

Reader: "This card is in the Mars position, which can refer to the masculine principle or simply to the actions we must take in order to achieve our goals."

Jenny: "Action. That's pretty clear. I have to use the sword, cut away the products that aren't thriving. There are a couple that I've been hanging on to, even though they don't sell well. Then I can move ahead. Expand."

Reader: "You can take off this stuff and come back to the table now. Another card?"

Jenny turns over the High Priestess card.

Card Seven: The High Priestess in the Earth Position

Jenny: "Goodness. What's this mean?"

Reader: "You tell me. What kind of person do we have in this card?"

Jenny: "Uh, wise, and spiritual, and . . . very centered, very connected. But she's a priestess—what does that have to do with my business?"

Reader: "Let's find out. Why did you start your business in the first place?"

Jenny: (Thinks silently for a moment.) "It wasn't just to make money. I wanted to help people live better, using beautiful and healthful things that wouldn't poison them or hurt the planet. I was appalled by the nasty chemicals in the popular skin lotions and shampoos and so on, and I thought I could create something better."

Reader: "And do you still feel that way?"

Jenny: "Yes. But I admit I've gotten so wrapped up in the details of the business that sometimes I forget the real purpose. When I started I was more focused, more passionate; it was like a sacred mission or something."

Reader: (Pointing at the card.) "Do you still wonder what a priestess has to do with your business?"

Jenny: "What is that card? I mean, what position is it in?"

Reader: "It's in the Earth position, the Self. It's you, Jenny."

Jenny: "Me. You mean . . . my business is like a holy calling? I'm like the priestess of herbal products? But I'm not like her, I'm not wise and totally spiritual."

Reader: "The Earth card symbolizes you at this time in your life, most closely of all the cards in the deck."

Jenny: "Oh. But I'm feeling a . . . a conflict, here. Do I approach my business as a spiritual person or as a hard-headed, competent, effective business-woman?"

Reader: "Is there a conflict between being spiritual and being competent and effective?"

Jenny: (Laughs.) "I see what you mean. No, of course not. The best spiritual leaders would be the most capable ones. So I guess this card is reminding me that there's a deeper purpose to my business, and that I shouldn't lose sight of the reasons I started it in the first place."

Reader: "You are the High Priestess of your business. Shall we go on?"

Jenny turns over the Five of Wands.

Card Eight: Five of Wands in the Moon Position

Jenny: "That's different. There's this confused jumble of hands and sticks. It looks like these guys are fighting, all brawling with sticks."

Reader: "Why are they fighting?"

Jenny: "Because, because they don't agree on what to do. They've got something to decide and instead of talking it out together like calm and rational people, they're losing their tempers and beating each other up."

Reader: "What's the issue?"

Jenny: "I think they want to build something with the sticks, but they can't agree on how to do it."

Reader: "What would happen if they could agree on the issue?"

Jenny: "Well, then they could all cooperate and build their project in no time. I mean, they're probably all mature, strong adults; they can do whatever they want if they stop wasting their energy beating each other up."

Reader: "Do you know anyone who can't decide what to do, so they beat up somebody?"

Jenny: "Well, I can't decide what to do, but I would never—oh. I do beat somebody up. Me. I've been raking myself over the coals because I couldn't figure out this expansion stuff."

Reader: "And if you stop beating yourself up?"

Jenny: "Then I could get on with building the business."

Reader: "How about another card?"

Jenny turns over the Eight of Cups.

Card Nine: Eight of Cups in the Mercury Position

Jenny: "I don't understand this one. Here is a cloaked figure, in the night, and he or she is walking away from all these cups or goblets."

Reader: "What is the figure thinking about, do you suppose?"

Jenny: "I don't know. Work, daily stuff. But it bothers me that she's ignoring these golden cups."

Reader: "What would you have her do?"

Jenny: "Well, she should pay attention. Then she would notice all these gold objects that someone has left lying around, and apparently no one else has noticed or they would have grabbed them. It's a treasure—she could be rich!"

Reader: "Do you want to be rich?"

Jenny: "Well, yes. Not to buy clothes and jewelry and all that, but there are a lot of causes I would like to support—mostly environmental and alternative health things. And I would like to buy land, and use part for growing more organic herbs and part as a wildlife sanctuary."

Reader: "Do you suppose you have ever missed some opportunities for wealth that were just lying around for someone to grab them?"

Jenny: "I'm not sure. I'm certainly not getting rich, so maybe I have missed something. But I do love my work."

Reader: "Think about it. Opportunities for wealth. It's dark outside, so you may not see them immediately. But there is moonlight, so it's not totally dark; look carefully, you might see something you almost walked past."

Jenny: "Mmmm. My friend David goes to an annual conference for New Age products; he asked once if I had ever thought about going. Apparently some of the big chains look for new product lines there."

Reader: "What else"

Jenny: "My cousin's a model. Actually she's pretty famous, so I guess that makes her a supermodel. She likes my stuff, and I bet she would give me a free endorsement."

Reader: "What else?"

Jenny: "I was offered free ad space in one of the big organic gardening magazines, if I would write a monthly column. I haven't really had time, so I haven't said yes or no yet."

Reader: "Do these qualify as opportunities for wealth, in the context of your business?"

Jenny: "Yeah, no doubt. I need to find time to do all this stuff and still make the products."

Reader: "Could anyone take over part of the manufacture?"

Jenny: "My younger sister said that she and several friends were looking for summer jobs. I guess with training they could do a lot of it, and they wouldn't cost a whole lot. Once they were trained, I could probably do more of this marketing stuff."

Reader: "This card is in the Mercury position. That's communication, among other things. I always think of it as a telegram from your deep mind, to help you notice something especially important."

Jenny: "I think the message here is that there are lots of opportunities around, but I've got to pay attention, follow up on them, and get some help for the routine work."

Reader: "Ready to move on?"

Jenny turns over the Seven of Cups.

Card Ten: Seven of Cups in the Pluto Position

Jenny: "Look at all this. It looks like an abundance of wealth, and resources, filling all the cups."

Reader: "The same cups you almost walked past?"

Jenny: "I suspect so. But look, some of the cups have good stuff like castles and victory wreaths, and some have scary stuff."

Reader: "Going back to the earlier card, with the golden cups in the night. How could you know which cups would have great stuff, and which wouldn't?"

Jenny: "I don't think you could be sure, not in the darkness. But the moon was up, so maybe you could see something."

Reader: "What does the moon symbolize to you?"

Jenny: "Intuition, instinct. I suppose if I trust my instincts, I could pick the right cups."

Reader: "This card is the Pluto position. Beginnings, endings, foundations, boundaries. Kind of a summing-up of the key issue underneath the whole question."

Jenny: "The key that I understand from this is that there are tons of resources and possibilities out there, good and bad. It's just a matter of making choices and plunging ahead."

Reader: "We're on the home stretch. Pick another card?"

Jenny turns over the Four of Pentacles.

Card Eleven: Four of Pentacles in the Vesta Position

Jenny: "Here's somebody who's gt a death grip on his stuff. He's not poor, but he's hanging on like it was his last four dimes."

Reader: "What do you think he's feeling?"

Jenny: "Greed. No, maybe not greed. He just doesn't have all that much, even if he is a king, and he's afraid to let go of any of it."

Reader: "It's his stuff, presumably. He can hold on to it if he wants."

Jenny: "Yes, but if he's concerned about his wealth, he should know that he'll never make any more by clutching this so tightly. My grandfather used to say that 'It takes money to make money.' Gramps was willing to risk his money for a return on his investment."

Reader: "How did your grandfather do on his investments?"

Jenny: "Pretty well. He didn't just fling his money around, he was smart about where he put it, and sometimes it didn't work out. But mostly he did all right."

Reader: "So you would advise this guy to stop clutching his pennies and make some intelligent investments? Take a few risks?"

Jenny: "Oh ho, it's me isn't it? I hope I'm not quite that tight with money, though!"

Reader: "The Tarot doesn't say you are. This is the Vesta position—'the unknown factor.' It's the one variable that can change the whole outcome of the reading—either a monkey wrench in the works, or a stroke of serendipity where everything works out better than you dreamed."

Jenny: (Slowly.) "So the question is, can I take risks and invest some of my money in the business to expand it, or will I sit and clutch what I've got? That's the variable everything depends on?"

Reader: "If you say so; you're the expert on you."

Jenny: "That's worth thinking about. I haven't put much capital into the company since I started it; maybe it's time. I'll do the last card." (Turns over the Nine of Cups.)

Card Twelve: The Nine of Cups in the Neptune Position

Reader: "What's the story with this person?"

Jenny: "A fat and sassy merchant. Look at all the gold cups, and that grin on his face. He's made out like a bandit."

Reader: "This is a successful merchant?"

Jenny: "Successful financially, quite well-fed, and obscenely happy. If the cups were opportunities, he's snarfled up every one."

Reader: "Perhaps we don't have to belabor this one. It's the Neptune position, 'future, prophecy, or outcome.'"

Jenny: "And the question was about expanding my business. Looks like a good move—if I remember some of the other messages in the reading. Is that it? Are we done?"

Reader: "Not quite. We want to look for patterns in the reading, and review what you've learned."

Jenny: "Oh, that sounds like a good idea."

Looking for Patterns

Reader: "Please look at the whole spread now, and tell me if you see any patterns, things which occur over and over, colors, shapes—anything at all."

Jenny: "Well, the first thing I notice is that there's this person on the far left clutching their stuff, hoarding it . . . and this other person on the far right who has his stuff out on the table, and a lot more of it."

Reader: "What does that contrast suggest to you?"

Jenny: "That if you hoard your stuff, don't make investments or take risks, you are going to wind up less prosperous down the road."

Reader: "What other patterns do you notice?"

Jenny: "I notice that most of the cards show single individuals. Only one shows a group, the Five of Wands, and that was an internal emotional thing."

Reader: "Do you like to work by yourself?"

Jenny: "Yeah, I do. This business has been my baby from the beginning, Pand I've done all the production, marketing, paperwork—everything.

Nobody else has been involved—well, to be honest I haven't let them become involved."

Reader: "Why is that?"

Jenny: "Mmmm. . . . Partly because I have strong ideas on how things should be done. I worry about somebody else messing it up, not doing it as well or as carefully as I would. And partly because I have trouble asking others for help. I just don't like to ask for things for myself. Alex, my husband, says I'm a giver not a taker—but to a ridiculous extreme."

Reader: "So how does this affect the possibility of expanding your business?"

Jenny: "Duh; it seems so obvious now—I can't expand it unless I'm willing to ask for help, share the workload, and trust others to do a good job. If I want to see what's held me back, I just have to look in the mirror."

Reader: "Anything else you notice, looking at the whole spread?"

Jenny: "Umn . . . both the King and Queen of Swords are here. That strikes me as significant somehow."

Reader: "What do swords mean to you? What do you associate with them."

Jenny: "Strength. Decisiveness. Cutting through red tape and nonsense, cutting out unnecessary stuff. I get this feeling of action, movement, very clean and crisp and powerful."

Reader: "Do you find those qualities in yourself?"

Jenny: "When I've got a clear goal, once I make a decision and commit, yes. I can be the King or Queen of Swords. I can be very strong and energetic."

Reader: "Any other patterns or recurring elements?"

Jenny: "Let's see . . . there are a lot of cups. Four cards with cups. Is that normal?"

Reader: "It's slightly more than average. On the average we might expect to see three of any given suit. What do cups suggest to you?"

Jenny: "Prosperity. Abundance. 'My cup runneth over.' Resources in general."

Reader: "And in the context of your original question?"

Jenny: "I asked about expanding the business. It looks to me like that could be a very profitable thing. If I use the resources available!"

Reader: "Anything else, or shall I summarize what we've discussed?"

Jenny: "I feel like so much has come out of this, so much knowledge and insight, I bet I've forgotten half of it. Please do sum it up, if you can."

Reader: "Well, I jotted some notes as we went along. You're welcome to take a copy with you, but let me try to hit the highlights:

"The King of Swords represents your source of power. You have focus and drive, combined with wisdom and foresight—good qualities for an entrepreneur!

"The World is your relationships. You said you've been so focused on your products that you haven't paid much attention to the customers, retailers, or anything much outside your workshop.

"The Two of Cups represents change. Your working relationship with your retailers may change, if you don't keep an eye on what the competition is doing.

"The Moon is things in your favor. You recognize the pond—your market—is too small, but you've been afraid to venture out of it. The dogs are your fears: of failure, of expanding, of responsibility, of success. Yet despite those fears, you're ready to come out and try something new.

"The Tower is obstacles. You have been confining your business to a few products in a few local stores, because you were afraid to expand. You felt safer limiting yourself.

"The Queen of Swords represents action. You need to look clearly and fearlessly at your business, use the sword, cut away the products that aren't thriving, be forceful and direct."

Jenny: "I really liked dressing up as the Queen."

Reader: "And you are the Queen, but you are also the High Priestess, who reminds you that there's a deeper purpose to your business: that it's a calling, a spiritual pursuit, and not just a money thing.

"The Five of Wands is your emotional state; you've been beating yourself up because the business wasn't going anywhere and you didn't know if you wanted to expand.

"The Eight of Cups is a message from your deep mind. You have overlooked some opportunities for wealth, some resources that have been staring you in the face: your cousin the model, the big products conference, your sister and her friends as a labor force, the column in the gardening magazine.

"The Seven of Cups represents the bottom-line issues. You have lots of resources and possibilities around you, and you can trust your intuition to pick the right ones.

"The Four of Pentagrams is the unknown factor, which is whether you will hoard your present resources and sit on the company as it is, or whether you will risk some resources and try something new.

"The Nine of Cups is the future, or at least the potential future if you decide to expand and do it intelligently. It's also prosperity and satisfaction."

Jenny: "It looks very favorable."

Reader: "And then there are the patterns, which suggest four things. First, that hoarding your money and refusing to take risks will not lead to expansion or prosperity.

"Second, that you have been pretty much working alone, and that expansion means you will have to be willing to involve and trust others.

"Third, that you have the capacity to be strong and take decisive action, which will be necessary for expansion.

"And fourth, that there are resources all around, and the potential for prosperity is high."

Jenny: "That's all pretty clear, and feels exactly right-on."

Reader: "Remember, the Tarot shows us what's happened in the past and what's going on now, and we can extrapolate what will probably happen if certain actions are taken, but there are no guarantees. The future is yours to shape, and is infinitely mutable."

Jenny: "I know. I understand that it depends on me, and of course on some other factors that can't be predicted exactly. But this has clarified a lot for me, and I think I can make some good decisions now."

Reader: "I wish you all the luck in the world, but I suspect you'll make your own. I have these printed sheets that show the Gestalt Spread; do you want to copy the cards you chose onto it, so you can take it home and recreate the reading?"

Jenny: "I don't think so, but I would like a copy of the notes you took. I think you got all the essentials down."

Reader: "Then I'll mail you a photocopy tomorrow, or do you have a fax?"

Jenny: "No, just mail them. Thank you so much. Is it okay if I pay you in cash?"

Reader: "Usually I prefer cattle or diamonds, but I guess I can make an exception."

Jenny: (Laughs.) "Here's your cash; next time I'll bring the cattle! I'll let you know what happens. Thanks again!"

Reader: "My pleasure. I'll walk you to the door."

Does every reading go like this one? Not at all. Every reading is different, and the variety is what makes reading Tarot for others endlessly fascinating.

Another Sample Reading

Here is another sample reading. This time Jason has come to you with a question: "Should Teresa and I get married?"

Well, relationship questions aren't that simple. A Gestalt Tarot reading isn't normally going to give you a blunt "yes" or "no." The Tarot can help you get a glimpse of what the relationship looks like now, where it might be headed, what some of the issues are that you might face as a couple, where the relationship will be strong and where it will be weak, and so on.

Given all that, Jason is going to have to decide whether to pop the question. Then Teresa may say yes or no. Further, both she and Jason may change over time, as far as what they want in a marriage and what they are willing to give. Outside pressures such as career and relatives may have an impact. The addition of children to the equation will certainly affect the relationship.

If a client comes to you hoping for a simple answer and a guarantee of happiness-ever-after, part of your job as reader will be to remind them that human relationships are messy, complex, and hard work to maintain. Otherwise they may hear what they want to in the reading and become angry with you when the relationship doesn't work out neatly. Let's listen in on the conversation:

Reader: "So you would like to know whether you and Teresa should marry. Normally I like to have both parties present when we're talking about a relationship. Any chance that you could come in together?"

Jason: "Actually we were going to. Then at the last minute Teresa had to work today. I suggested that we postpone it, but she told me to go

Sample Gestalt Tarot Reading

161

ahead, that if it was really helpful then we could both come back another time. (Smiles.) What she said was, 'Check it out and see if it's baloney or not.' No offense."

Reader: "None taken. Have you ever had a Tarot reading before?"

Jason, as Querent: "Yes, once a long time ago. I don't remember much about it, but I seem to remember it was pretty right-on."

Reader: "Let me explain a little about Tarot. First, you should understand that a reading won't tell you what you and Teresa *should* do. It can help you understand the relationship and where it's headed, but it can't guarantee the success or failure of a marriage. That depends on two human beings who both have free will. So we can get some good insights, but I'm not going to pretend that there will be a simple answer."

Jason: "Okay, that makes sense. But anything you can tell me will help."

Reader: "The second thing I want to mention is that I use a method of Tarot reading called Gestalt Tarot. That means I will be asking you a lot of questions about the cards, and the information we get is going to come out of your deep mind, not mine. It's more work for you than if I just spout a bunch of stuff, but I've found that it's more accurate and meaningful than other methods."

Jason: "So you ask me questions? I don't understand—how will I know the answers? And why would I need a Tarot reading if I had the answers already?"

Reader: "You have the answers, but not in your conscious mind. They're in your subconscious, and my job is to help you bring them to the surface. I have some good ways to do that."

Jason: "All right. What do we do next?"

Reader: "As I mentioned over the phone, I charge $40 for a reading, and the reading will last about an hour. You can pay me at the end of the reading, okay?" (Jason nods.) "Now let's get acquainted with the cards. Here's the deck I use: it's called the *Morgan-Greer* deck, and I use it because I like the artwork and the colors. Why don't you look through the deck a little bit?"

Jason: "Okay." (Quietly looks through the deck for a minute.)

162

Sample

Tarot

Readings

Reader: "Now think about your relationship with Teresa as you shuffle the cards a few times. . . . Now, if you would, divide them into three stacks, then put them back together in whatever order feels right."

Jason does so.

Reader: "Right. Now take the cards one at a time and put them face-down on the diagram here. You can take them from the top of the deck or from inside. Just put each card wherever it feels right; don't think about it too much."

Jason: "Just wherever it feels right?"

Reader: "Yes. Trust your feelings."

Jason: (Hesitantly places each card.) "Is that okay?"

Reader: "Perfect. Now you can turn over any card. We'll look at that one and then turn over each of the others, one at a time."

Jason turns over the Page of Rods.

Card One: Page of Rods in the Sun Position

Reader: "What's the first thing you notice about this card?"

Jason: "He's got a funny hat. Like a derby with a feather."

Reader: "Is he a funny person?"

Jason: "No, I didn't mean that. He seems like a very thoughtful person."

Reader: "What else can you tell about him?"

Jason: "Uh—he travels a lot. He's got this hiking staff—it looks like he's out in the wilderness. He's somebody who likes to keep on the move."

Reader: "Can you describe his personality to me?"

Jason: "I think he's thoughtful, knows where he's going and how to get there, likes to travel light and fast; very competent and efficient."

Reader: "This card is in the Sun position, which is also called the 'Power Source.' This is what you draw your personal strength from at this time in your life."

Jason: "Could you explain a little more?"

Reader: "You draw strength from thinking things out, then moving as quickly and efficiently as you can toward your goal. Travel, movement, change, these all seem to be things that motivate you."

Jason: "I guess you got that right. My dad calls me 'a rolling stone.'"

Reader: "Keep these things in mind as we look at the rest of the cards. You can turn over another card if you like."

Jason turns over the Lovers card.

Card Two: The Lovers in the Earth Position

Jason: "Hah, it's practically X-rated."

Reader: "Tell me about these people. What are they feeling?"

Jason: "Well, obviously they're feeling pretty good about each other. They're both very serious, but I think it's a good serious."

Reader: "What do you suppose the man is thinking?"

Jason: "Ah . . . he's probably not thinking about Monday night football."

Reader: "Apart from sex, what does he feel about her?"

Jason: "He's feeling very protective, very tender, very respectful. He's very focused on her, and she's very, very important to him. I could imagine him going off to work or hunt or something, but it's like he would always want to come back to her."

Reader: "So she's like a center or an anchor for him? The person he comes home to?"

Jason: "Yeah, that's it exactly."

Reader: "How do you think they get along when they're together?"

Jason: "Well, they love each other."

Reader: "I got that. But sometimes people love each other and still don't understand each other, or agree on things, or communicate well."

Jason: "True. But I think these people do. She's a redhead, I'll bet she has strong opinions; and he's no wimp. But I think they care enough to really work things out if there's a problem."

Reader: "This card is in the Earth position. It represents you at this time in your life."

Jason: "Hmmm. It looks like I'm really ready for the relationship thing."

Reader: "Does that make sense to you?"

Jason: "Yes. Yes, it does. I haven't lost my wanderlust, but I'm thinking more and more how great it would be to have someone, and to make a home together. Not that I want to totally settle down and never travel, but I want more than just that."

Reader: "Want to try another card?"

Jason moves straight down the row and turns over the Queen of Cups.

Card Three: Queen of Cups in the Moon Position

Reader: "What did you notice first?"

Jason: "Well, she's got this big gold cup, and she's just about to take a big swig of whatever's in it."

Reader: "What else can you tell me about her?"

Jason: "She's a queen, she's royalty. Very calm and confident-looking. But she's got this big shell, I don't know, like a shield behind her. Maybe to protect herself from the ocean?"

Reader: "Why would she need protection from the ocean?"

Jason: "Well, the ocean is huge and powerful, and there are a lot of hazards in it . . . you know, sharks and currents and storms and all. Personally I love the ocean, but I can see how it might scare some people."

Reader: "Even an otherwise confident queen?"

Jason: "Sure. Everybody's scared of something."

Reader: "This card is in the Moon position, which refers to emotional position. Do you know anyone this card might describe?"

Jason: "That's not easy. I know Tarot cards sometimes refer to the person the reading's about . . . well, Teresa is a confident person, but I think she is a little bit scared or protective of herself at the same time."

Reader: "The queen is scared of the ocean. What is Teresa scared of? What is the ocean for her?"

Jason: "Love. Passion. Commitment. At least that's what I think. I know she cares for me a lot, but sometimes when the conversation gets intense she gets nervous and changes the subject."

Reader: "Something else is on your mind about this card."

Jason: "Yeah. I also said that the queen is all ready to drink from the goblet, and that's kind of contradictory. I'm not sure Teresa really is. Ready for commitment, I mean."

Reader: "Are you?"

Jason: "I think so. I'm pretty sure of it. But if the queen is Teresa . . . ?"

Reader: "There's no law that says the queen can only represent one person. Look at her again. Ignore the gender, is there any of you in there?"

Jason: "Oh. Yes. Because I am ready to take that swig, to dive in. So the shielded part is Teresa, and the part that's ready to go for it is me. Interesting."

Reader: "Another card?"

Jason turns over the Eight of Pentacles.

Card Four: The Eight of Pentacles in the Pluto Position

Reader: "What is this man doing?"

Jason: "Working really hard, making these things. What are they? He's finished a bunch of them, up on the wall."

Reader: "They're called pentacles. What's he thinking? What's he feeling?"

Jason: "He's really focused. I mean, he's going to town making these things, just digging in. I think he's liking the work, feeling good about what he's making."

Reader: "Do you suppose he's always been like this, really focused and enjoying his work?"

Jason: "I don't know. If I had to guess, I'd say no; he was a swingin' dude who wandered around and tried out different stuff. But now he's found something he really likes and he's zeroed in on it."

Reader: "This is in the Pluto position, which is a little hard to describe. We call it 'beginnings, endings, outer boundaries.' You could also call it the parameters of the situation, or the bottom line. It answers the question, 'What's this situation all about, anyway?'"

Jason: "So this is all about . . . me finding something—someone—I really like and settling down?"

Reader: "'A swingin' dude who wandered around . . . now he's found something he really likes.' Is that you?"

Jason: "Probably so. Probably so. But that's me. Just because I'm ready for marriage and all doesn't mean Teresa is, or that it would work out between us."

Reader: "Sounds like a very important point. You need to know whether marriage is what just you want, or whether Teresa wants it too, and whether it's a good match, regardless of who wants it."

Jason: "Right. Can I turn over another card?"

Reader: "Please."

Jason turns over the Ace of Rods.

Card Five: Ace of Rods in the Vesta Position

Jason: "I have no clue what this means. A hand is coming out of the clouds and holding a tree. Well, a stick—it's cut off but it still has leaves on it."

Reader: "We saw a stick earlier, on the first card. What did it mean there?"

Jason: "It meant—like, travel and freedom. It was the walking stick this guy used on his journeys."

Reader: "Does this have a similar meaning?"

Jason: "It could, except it's cut short. It's too short to be a hiking staff, if it was."

Reader: "A hiking staff cut short? What might that mean?"

Jason: "Uh, freedom, travel, cut short. . . . . Oh. It means that if I get married I won't be free just to take off anytime and go where I please. I'll have Teresa to think about."

Reader: "How would being married to Teresa curtail your freedom, your trips?"

Jason: "Well, her job doesn't let her get away as easily as mine does. And some day there might be kids, which definitely affects the picture. But she does like to travel almost as much as I do, and she's fun to travel with. So I don't think I would have to give it up entirely."

Reader: "This is the Vesta card, sometimes called the "Unknown factor." It symbolizes key things that could change the whole situation— monkey wrenches—or strokes of good luck."

Jason: "So . . . cutting back on my travel, or my freedom, might change the whole picture?"

Reader: "Apparently it could. I guess the question is, 'If your freedom and your travel were cut back, would that wreck the marriage as far as you're concerned?'"

Jason: "I don't think so. But I'm not sure. I guess I'm going to have to think more about that."

Reader: "Good idea. Do you want to turn over another one?"

Jason turns over the Queen of Swords.

Card Six: Queen of Swords in the Jupiter Position

Jason: "Another queen! What's that about?"

Reader: "We'll find out. Now imagine that she's looking you right in the eye, and that she speaks to you. What does she say?"

Jason: "Mmmm. She's saying, 'I've got these flowers and maybe you can share my roses, but if you mess with me I'll take your head off.'"

Reader: "She sounds—fierce."

Jason: "Oh yeah. Strong lady. Roses but also thorns; and that sword is the biggest thorn of all."

Reader: "How do you feel about this kind of woman?"

Jason: "Really attracted. I like strong women, could never stand wimpy types."

Reader: "What would be the advantages of being linked up with a woman like this?"

Jason: "You mean married, or working together? Well, she would pull her weight in whatever you did together. She would be competent, capable. You could both get farther in life, working as a team, and you wouldn't constantly have to be worrying about her. Some guys like the helpless type, but I'd rather be with an adult."

Reader: "Okay, so who is this woman?"

Jason: "It's got to be Teresa. Teresa's a lot like this; well, a lot like the Queen of Cups too, but this is even more her style. It even looks kind of like her. It's funny, Teresa even likes roses. Red roses!"

Reader: "This card is in the Jupiter position, 'Things in Your Favor.' I think that speaks for itself."

Jason: "Absolutely. I'll do another card now." (Turns over the Ten of Cups.)

Card Seven: Ten of Cups in the Mercury Position

Reader: "What's the feeling you get from this picture?"

Jason: "Happiness. As in, 'They lived happily ever after.' Rainbow, his and her arms intertwined, beautiful scenery in the background. There's probably a rose-covered cottage just outside the picture, with a dog named 'Spot' and a kitten named 'Fluff.'"

Reader: "You sound a little—cynical? Disbelieving?"

Jason: "I just don't think it's that easy, or that there are storybook happy endings."

Reader: "This is in the Mercury position, representing 'Message' or 'Thought.' I sometimes think of it as a message from your deep mind to your conscious mind."

Jason: "So my deep mind is telling me that Teresa and I are going to live happily ever after?"

Reader: "Do you see you and Teresa in that picture?"

Jason: "I want to. I really do. And sometimes, it feels that way, like that could be us. But then Teresa backs away. So I guess I'm a little scared to believe it could really happen."

Reader: "So what is your deep mind telling you?"

Jason: "That it is possible. Not to give up hope. The rainbow says there's a lot of hope in this picture."

Reader: "Do you want to look at another card?"

Jason: "Sure." (Turns over the Eight of Rods.)

Card Eight: Eight of Rods in the Uranus Position

Jason: "What is this? A bunch of sticks, or staves, flying through the air, I guess."

Reader: "What's your first impression of this picture?"

Jason: "Ummm . . . movement. From right to left, like bars being pulled aside. Yeah, like these poles were across the picture, barring the way, and now they're being withdrawn."

Reader: "Close your eyes for a moment. Now imagine the bars in place, like they were, right in front of you, keeping you out."

Jason: (Closing his eyes.) "Got it. Don't like it, but I can imagine it."

Reader: "Now here's a question: does this feel familiar? Have you felt that recently, or not?"

Jason: "It's familiar, all right. That's how I've felt about Teresa—stuck, held back, can't get anywhere."

Reader: "Now look at the card."

Jason: (Opens his eyes.) "Right, the bars are pulling back, and there's this beautiful landscape on the other side."

Reader: "This card is in the Uranus position, which represents changes in the situation. What else do you see in the card?"

Jason: "Well, there are green leaves sprouting from the sticks. That's a hopeful sign to me."

Reader: "What else? Put yourself in the landscape; be there on the shore of the river."

Jason: "I notice these big, towering clouds. Thunderheads. That's odd."

Reader: "What's odd?"

Jason: "Before, when the barrier was there, all I could think of was getting past it, and how perfect it would be on the other side. Now the barrier's gone and I'm there, and . . . well, it's still this beautiful green place, but I'm also feeling a cool breeze and seeing these storm clouds coming in. It's not as perfect as I thought."

Reader: "So you can sum up the changes happening here?"

Jason: "The barrier is going away, which I think means that Teresa and I might actually get together. But when we do, it's not totally perfect. There are still those clouds."

Reader: "How scary are those clouds, or should I say the storm that's coming in?"

Jason: "Not totally scary. Not like a total disaster, just wind and rain for a while."

Reader: "And what happens after the storm?"

Jason: "Afterwards? Well, I guess the sun comes out again, and the fields are even greener, and everything's okay."

Reader: "How about choosing another card?"

Jason turns over the Temperance card.

Card Nine: Temperance in the Mars Position

Jason: "Okay, here's this angel dude, and he's standing by a lake or something, and pouring water back and forth between these cups."

Reader: "What's he thinking about, do you suppose?"

Jason: "About pouring the water, probably. Trying not to spill it."

Reader: "And what's his mood? What is he feeling?"

Jason: "I haven't got a clue."

Reader: "Wait just a second. (Leaves, and returns with two large wine goblets. One is filled with water.) Please stand up, and hold one of these in each hand."

Jason: (Stands and takes the goblets.) "Okay."

Reader: "Now imagine that you are the Angel of Temperance. You're standing by the lake, your great golden wings are spread, and begin pouring the water slowly back and forth. Go ahead."

Jason begins to carefully pour the water back and forth. Soon he has a steady rhythm going.

Reader: "Keep pouring, and tell me how you feel."

Jason: (In a quiet, almost dreamy voice.) "Peaceful. Very focused, very balanced. Calm. I can feel my wings expanding in the air and the sunlight, and the ground under my feet, and there's the water flowing, and I'm the center of it all."

Reader: "Okay, you can stop now before you pour it on the rug."

Jason: (Laughs.) "That was neat. So peaceful."

Reader: (Takes the goblets.) "Have a seat. That card is in the Mars position, which shows the action you need to take to make things work out for the best."

Jason: "But all I did was stand there and pour water."

Reader: "That's not all you did. You got into a very calm, centered place, mentally and emotionally."

Jason: "Well, yeah. So I guess all I need to do is be calm and balanced with Teresa."

Reader: "What are the alternatives?"

Jason: "Well, I could keep pushing her for an answer. No, that's just going to make it worse. I think I see. I need to stay calm and let her come around when she's ready."

Reader: "Turn over another card, if you're ready."

Jason turns over the Four of Pentacles.

Card Ten: Four of Pentacles of the Venus Position

Jason: "Hey, that's strange. This guy has the same look as the last one, the angel."

Reader: "What do you mean?"

Jason: "See, he's really calm and centered and peaceful. He's a king, not an angel, but he's got the same feel to him."

Reader: "I see what you mean. What else can you tell me about the card?"

Jason: "He's holding these big pentacles, and he's got a stone wall behind him."

Reader: "How does he feel about the stone wall?"

Jason: "Not a problem. It's behind him; it's not blocking his way. It's more like a symbol of strength and solidity."

Reader: "And what do these pentacles mean to you?"

Jason: "They stand for balance. This king is totally strong, and balanced, and stable."

Reader: "What would you say if I told you that this is the Venus position, which stands for love and relationships?"

Jason: "Oh. Hm. But there's only one person in the card."

Reader: "Why is that?"

Jason: "Because—well, maybe because there's a wall there. The king is very calm, cool, and collected as long as he's by himself, with the big wall between him and anybody else. But he can't exactly have a relationship there by himself."

Reader: "Why did he go behind the wall?"

Jason: "'Cause he's got his life together alone, it's safe and predictable, and if he took down the wall he might lose all that."

Reader: "And who is this king?"

Jason: "Me, I guess . . . no, that can't be. Oh! It's not a king! It's Teresa again, she's a queen. It even looks like Teresa, even more than that other queen."

Reader: "So what does this tell you about Teresa and your relationship?"

Jason: "That Teresa still has some walls up—I think I knew that—to keep her life safe and stable. That we're not going to have much of a relationship until she decides to bring that wall down."

Reader: "And what can you do to bring the wall down?" (Points to the Temperance card.)

Jason: "Hah! Not much. Be patient, be calm, be centered. At least I understand a little better why she keeps that wall up. It must be scary for her. Making a commitment to me would change everything."

Reader: "There are still a couple more cards."

Jason turns over the Two of Pentacles.

Card Eleven: Two of Pentacles in the Saturn Position

Jason: "Oh god, it's Teresa again."

Reader: "How do you think she's feeling in this card?"

Jason: "She looks a little worried. I guess she's trying to balance these pentacles and she's not sure she can do it."

Reader: "In this other card, you did say that pentacles represent balance."

Jason: "Yes. And in the other card (points to the Four of Pentacles), she's got them balanced, under control. Here they're not."

Reader: "What's different about this card, besides the pentacles?"

Jason: "Well, there's the ocean back here—that's it! The wall's down. Now there's wind and waves and it's harder to keep the things balanced."

Reader: "What did you say the ocean was about, up here?" (Points to the Queen of Cups.)

Jason: "Let's see . . . about commitment, and marriage, and being involved."

Reader: "Let me see if I understand what you're saying. She lets the wall down, opens herself up to the idea of marriage, and now she's worried and having trouble staying in balance?"

Jason: "Exactly."

Reader: "This card is in the Saturn position. It's about obstacles."

Jason: "Of course. Teresa knows that her world will be turned upside down if she gets married, and she's nervous about that. I don't blame her. If marriage had come up for me even three or four years ago, I would have been a little freaked at the idea."

Reader: "The two hats are really different; I mean the queen's crown over here (points to the Four of Pentacles), and the red hat with the feather here."

Jason: "Hmm. Over here, behind the wall, she's the queen. She's in control of her world behind the wall. If the wall goes down, she's not the queen any more; she's not completely in control. This is more like a page's hat."

Reader: "A page. So how does a page feel?"

Jason: "I suppose sort of young and inexperienced, unsure of himself, just learning the ropes. And that's how Teresa must feel about marriage."

Reader: "One more card. Are you ready?"

Jason: "Sure." (Turns over the Nine of Rods.)

Card Twelve: Nine of Rods in the Neptune Position

Reader: "Tell me about this guy."

Jason: "He looks confident, strong, proud. He's got the red plumes and all; he's a knight or soldier."

Reader: "What is he doing?"

Jason: "Well, he's got a staff—more staffs!—and there are a bunch more behind him."

Reader: "Are these similar to the staffs up here, or different?" (Points to the Eight of Rods.)

Jason: "No, different. Those were a barrier, and horizontal. These are upright and I think the knight placed them there."

Reader: "Why would he place them there?"

Jason: "Building something? A stockade or a wall?"

Reader: "Different or similar to the wall here?" (Points to the Four of Pentacles.)

Jason: "Oh, way different. That wall is stone, really heavy-duty. It blocks everything. This wall or whatever is like a boundary, but you can see right through it. It's open and light and the wind can blow right through."

Reader: "So here's a boundary instead of a stone wall. Interesting. What does that tell you about you and Teresa and her walls?"

Jason: (Thinking hard.) "That . . . maybe a boundary is a good thing. Maybe she needs that to feel safe and be the queen in her own domain. It doesn't have to be a big stone wall, but there needs to be something there."

Reader: "And what's your role in regard to this boundary?"

Jason: "To help her maintain it. To respect it." (Looks at the knight.) "To guard it for her. To be the guard instead of the guy battering away at the wall. The boundary. That looks like a real key to making it work for us."

Reader: "This card is in the Neptune position, which represents a prophecy or the future."

Jason: "But there's only me. Where's Teresa?"

Reader: "He knows." (Points at the knight.) "Go into his head. Be him. Here, stand up." (Gets a wooden staff from behind the door and hands it to Jason.) "Hold it in your left hand, over your shoulder. Now. You're wearing a silver helmet, red plume in it; red cloak, patrolling the boundary formed by these staves."

Jason: "Okay, okay, I've got it."

Reader: "Where's Teresa?"

Jason: "I think she's nearby. What's the point in a boundary unless she's there? Yes, I'm walking to meet her, there's an opening right up ahead."

Reader: "So the future is . . . ?"

Jason: "I believe we will be together, as long as I respect her boundaries, let her have her own space. That feels really right." (Pauses.) "Well, is that it?"

x

175

Sample

Tarot

Readings

Reader: "Not just yet. We need to look for patterns in the reading, and review what you've learned."

Jason: "Okay, let's do it."

Looking for Patterns

Reader: "Let's look at the whole spread now. Can you tell me if you see any patterns, things that occur over and over, colors, shapes, anything at all?"

Jason: "I guess the first thing is all those sticks—staves, rods, whatever you call them. There are four of them, mostly sort of arced along the top and sides."

Reader: "What do you think of when you look at them all?"

Jason: "They all have green leaves on them. Oak leaves, actually."

Reader: "And what do green leaves, oak leaves symbolize for you?"

Jason: "Growth. New beginnings. Something young and growing, and potentially very strong, since it's oaks. I've always liked oak trees."

Reader: "Let's relate this back to your question, which was originally 'Should I marry Teresa?' and which we've been approaching more as 'Tell me about the energies surrounding a marriage with Teresa.'"

Jason: "Well, it looks hopeful to me. Growing and potentially very strong."

Reader: "What other patterns do you notice?"

Jason: "Sort of right across the middle are these three queens. Let's see— a queen with pentacles, the Queen of Cups, and the Queen of Swords. They're sort of cupping the Lovers card."

Reader: "What does that suggest to you?"

Jason: "This will sound corny, but it's true. She's like the queen of my heart."

Reader: "Do you see any change or progression in the queens here, or are they all simply aspects of Teresa?"

Jason: "Both, probably. On the left she's really walled away and protected, in the middle she's only got a shell to shield her, then on the right she's this awesomely strong warrior queen."

Reader: "And what do you understand from that"

Jason: "I think this is the direction she's headed, how she's developing as a person, and obviously that has a pretty direct bearing on a marriage."

Reader: "So how does this particular pattern of growth affect the possibility of your marrying each other?"

Jason: "I think it's a very good thing. She's already wonderful and this means she's getting stronger and more open."

Reader: "Anything else you notice, looking at the whole spread?"

Jason: "Uh . . . three cards with pentacles on them. Quite a contrast between the Four of Pentacles and the Two of Pentacles. We already talked about that."

Reader: "We saw a pattern that seems to show a change or growth in Teresa. Do you see any pattern that applies to your own growth?"

Jason: "Okay, from the Page of Rods up here, to the Ace, and down to the Eight of Pentacles and over to the Nine of Rods. Hey, I'm all around the edges and Teresa's in the middle!"

Reader: "Interesting pattern. Why would it be like that?"

Jason: "Let's see . . . Teresa's in the middle of it all . . . maybe it means that she's the deciding factor in whether we'll get married? Well, yeah. I've already made up my mind, so it's kind of up to her."

Reader: "But you have some kind of effect on her decision?"

Jason: "Yes, I guess I must. Okay, I was the travelin' man up here (points to the Page of Rods), now I'm ready to settle down some (points to the Eight of Pentacles). As far as marrying Teresa, I've got to be calm and patient (points to Temperance), and . . . guard her boundaries (points to the Nine of Rods), protect her space. Maybe just back off a little; give her space."

Reader: "Sounds pretty wise to me. Anything else that catches your eye?"

Jason: "Just that I like these cards—the Ten of Cups and the Lovers. I'm real happy about those."

Reader: "Was your question answered?"

Jason: "I asked about marrying Teresa. It looks real positive—if I give it time and don't do anything stupid."

Reader: "There are no guarantees. And we're talking about a human being here, who has her own free will and must make her own decisions about what's best for her life. It sounds like you know what you want, now in time we'll see if that's what she wants."

Jason: "We covered a lot of ground. I don't know if I can remember all this stuff."

Reader: "I wrote some notes during the reading—mostly key phrases in your own words. You're welcome to take a copy with you."

Jason: "That would be great."

Reader: "And here is a copy of the Gestalt Tarot Spread. I've marked in the cards you picked, so you can re-create the reading if you have a Tarot deck."

Jason: "Cool. I don't have a deck, but I think I might get one. This has been really helpful; I wish Teresa had been here."

Reader: "Come back in a while with her, if she wants to have a joint reading. Chances are you'll discover even more about the two of you."

Jason: "We might just do that. Well, this has been really good. I owe you some money—is a check okay?"

Reader: "That's fine."

Jason: "Thanks again!"

Reader: "Come back again. I'd love to meet Teresa."

Readings about relationships pose an ethical question. Normally you wouldn't do a reading about an individual, without their permission, at the request of a third party; that's obviously invading their privacy. However, if a client asks about a relationship, you can't very well do an intelligent reading without including discussion about both people.

Two approaches work. One is to say, "Yes. I'll do the reading with you, but it will focus on your role in the relationship, and not much on the other person."

The other is to say, "When I do readings about a couple's relationship, I like to have both of you present if possible." This removes any privacy issues and, by the way, provides a more balanced and complete reading.

This particular reading was an exception to these policies. Upon assurance that Teresa was okay with the idea, the reader chose to go ahead with only Jason present.

Section III

⁎ | ⁎

The Compleat Tarot

Chapter 10

More
Spreads

The main Gestalt Spread presented in chapter 5 is traditional. However, Gestalt interpretive techniques can be used in any kind of spread. You may enjoy using some of the spreads shown here in this chapter.

Snapshot Spread

This is a handy little two-card spread that provides focus or guidance almost immediately. It can be a morning exercise to help you focus your mind for the day's activities ahead, a quick reference when you run into a puzzling situation, or a preliminary exercise to help you structure a longer, more complex reading.

Divide the deck into Major and Minor Arcana (remember, the Major Arcana are the first twenty-two cards; the Minor Arcana are all the rest of the cards, divided into Swords, Cups, Wands, and Pentacles). Then choose your question; it can be as broad as, "What's happening with me today?" or as specific as, "Why am I feeling angry at Jack right now?"

Then choose a card from the Major Arcana—either the top or from within the stack, whatever feels best. This represents a universal concept you're working on, or the issue underlying the situation you've asked about. This is the "what" card.

Now choose a card from the Minor Arcana. This one shows the best way for you to proceed. This is the "how" card.

With only two cards, you should have a better grasp of the situation and what to do about it. (Gail Fairfield shows a similar spread in her book *Choice Centered Tarot*, New York: Weiser, 1997, now newly released and titled *Everyday Tarot*.)

The Issue
(Major Arcanum)

What I Should Do About It
(Minor Arcanum)

The Snapshot Spread

The Three-Card Spread

This spread is based on the idea that there are "three aspects to every question and three choices of action: your current position, a new possibility or opposite action, and the integration of these two in a new way. . . . There are three choices, three levels of the Self, three aspects of time [past, present, and future]."

Shuffle the cards and divide them into three stacks, representing Body (your physical state), Mind (your attitudes and ideas), and Spirit (your ideals and goals). Interpret the cards using these categories, then go back and look at the same three cards as representing Past, Present, and Future . . . then Subconscious ("Younger Self"), Conscious ("Talking Head Self"), and Superconscious ("Higher Self"). Continue down the categories for as long as you find it useful. (Mary Katherine Greer originated a similar spread in *The Tarot Network News*, Winter 1983.)

| 1 | 2 | 3 |

Select from among the following categories, or create your own.

Body	Mind	Spirit
Past	Present	Future
Subconscious	Conscious	Superconscious
Child	Parent	Adult
Appearance	Reality	Possibility
Probable Outcome	Alternative	Change Agent
Beginning	Obstacle	Outcome
Active Principle	Receptive	Creative

The Three-Card Spread

Celtic Cross Spread

The Celtic Cross is one of the oldest and most popular spreads. The ten positions in the layout (see p. 185) are as follows:

1. What covers you: the current situation, general atmosphere, or what the querent is experiencing in regard to the question.

2. What crosses you: influences on the situation, or opposing forces, for good or ill.

3. What crowns you: the querent's conscious awareness of the situation.

4. What is beneath you: the basis of the situation; the origin or foundation of the question, or the subconscious feelings.

5. What is behind you: the past, an influence in the process of dissipating or leaving.

6. What is before you: the influence coming to bear in the near future.

7. Your strengths and weaknesses, and how you are creating your future.

8. The environment; feelings and influences of those around you: family, friends, and close associates.

9. Your hopes and fears about the situation or its potential outcome.

10. The outcome: the summation of all the other cards, and the long-term result.

Some traditions would have you choose a Significator to represent the client, before the actual layout of the spread. First choose the suit that corresponds to the question being asked: Rods for spiritual matters; Cups for emotional issues; Swords for questions about power, position, or authority; and Pentacles for monetary, job, health, or house matters.

Then choose a court card that symbolizes the client: the King for a mature man; the Queen for a mature woman; the Knight for a young man; or the Page for a youth or maiden.

The function of the Significator in traditional readings is not clear; however, in Gestalt it may be interpreted as you would any card in the spread, and it refers to the querent.

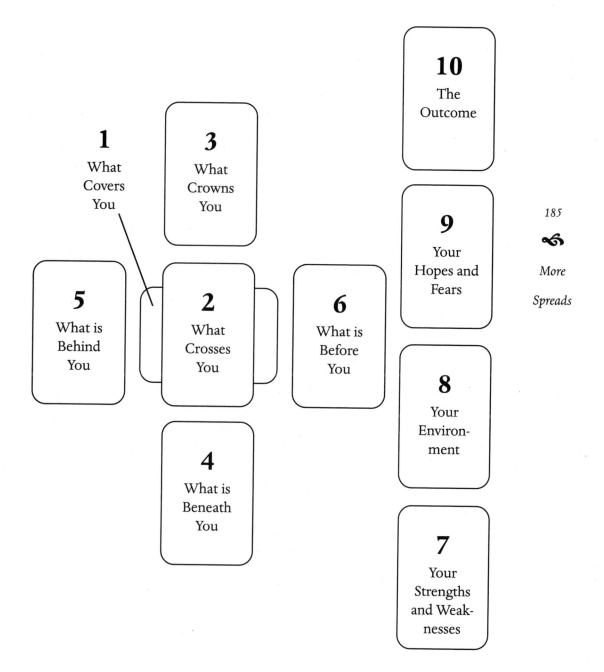

1
What
Covers
You

3
What
Crowns
You

10
The
Outcome

5
What is
Behind
You

2
What
Crosses
You

6
What is
Before
You

9
Your
Hopes and
Fears

8
Your
Environ-
ment

4
What is
Beneath
You

7
Your
Strengths
and Weak-
nesses

The Celtic Cross Spread

The Horoscope Spread

This is another traditional layout, tying the Tarot to astrology. Consider the question, shuffle, and lay out twelve cards in a circle as shown on the diagram, facedown. The cards represent the twelve houses in a horoscope, to wit:

- First House: key word BODY; Your physical self, health, appearance, personality, and self-expression—how you present yourself

- Second House: key word THINGS; Money, possessions, and personal resources; how you feel about resources and use them

- Third House: key word LEARNING; Immediate environment, relatives, neighbors, early learning, and communications

- Fourth House: key word HOME; Personal foundations, parents, conditions in your home, and psychological roots

- Fifth House: key word CREATIVITY; Your children, arts, hobbies, vocation, and entertainment

- Sixth House: key word WORK; Working conditions, relationships with those at work, service, craftsmanship, and career

- Seventh House: key word PARTNERS; Marriage, partnerships, how you relate to others who are close to you

- Eighth House: key words SEX and CHANGE; Sex, drastic change or transformation (including death), loss, regeneration, joint resources, and how you feel about these

- Ninth House: key word PHILOSOPHY; Beliefs, religion, science, higher education, understanding of the world

- Tenth House: key word STATUS; Your public image, reputation, attitude toward your community, and position in your profession

- Eleventh House: key word ASSOCIATIONS; Organizations you are part of and their goals, your hopes and dreams

- Twelfth House: key word CONSEQUENCES; The summation of your life experiences and contributions, integration, fulfillment

Beginning with the lower of the two left-hand cards (First House), turn over each card and interpret it, moving widdershins (counterclockwise).

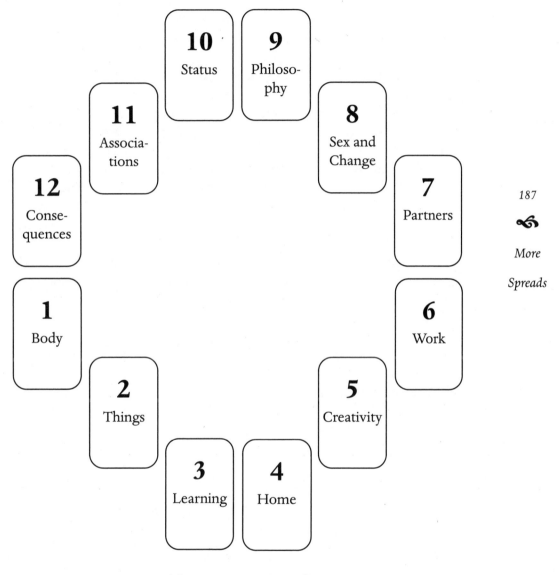

The Horoscope Spread

The Name Spread

Shuffle the deck as usual, while concentrating on the question to be asked. Then lay out the cards in three rows, with one card for each letter in the querent's first, middle, and last names.

Divide the first row into three sections; if there are an odd number of cards, then the middle section should include only one card; if an even number, put two in the middle section. Divide the second row likewise into three sections, and the third row into five sections. (If a name is shorter than the number of sections into which the row is to be divided, add more cards as needed on the right-hand end, but do not count these cards when determining the Age Card.)

Then interpret the cards according to their position in the spread. The sections in the top row represent the past, present, and future. The second row stands for obstacles, the self, and allies—what would be the Saturn, Earth, and Jupiter cards in a Gestalt layout. The last row represents the querent's body, mind, spirit, emotions, and will. (If the querent has no middle name, add a row of three cards below the last name and give it the middle name meanings. Ignore this row when counting for the Age Card. If the querent has two middle names, lay out cards for both names in the middle row.)

The name spread has one additional interesting feature: the Age Card. Starting at the top left, count out the querent's age card by card; if you run out of cards just go back to the top left and keep counting. The card you end on, the Age Card, is thought to be especially important to the whole question of the reading.

Stuart Kaplan does a variation of this spread in his book *Tarot Cards for Fun and Fortune Telling*.(U.S. Games)

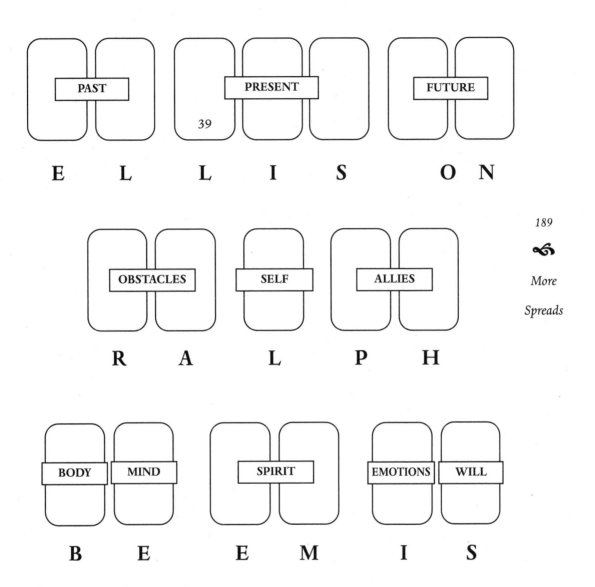

The Name Spread

The sample shown here is for Ellison Ralph Beemis, age 39.

The Comparison Spread

The Comparison Spread begins with one card at the left to establish the foundation or origin of the present situation. To its right are two more cards, the lower one representing the present situation, and the upper one representing the querent.

The next column represents the three most likely outcomes to the situation. Rarely is a future outcome carved in stone; we and all the other players in a given situation have free will, and our choices will, to a large degree, determine what happens.

The top card in this column shows the most probable outcome, assuming that no one involved does anything radically different than they are already doing or planning. The card below it is the next most likely outcome, and the bottom card is the least likely of the three—but still possible.

Once the querent has examined all three possibilities, using Gestalt methods, they should be ready to choose which one they would prefer to happen. At this point the querent draws one or more additional cards, up to three, to show the ACTION REQUIRED in order to bring about that outcome.

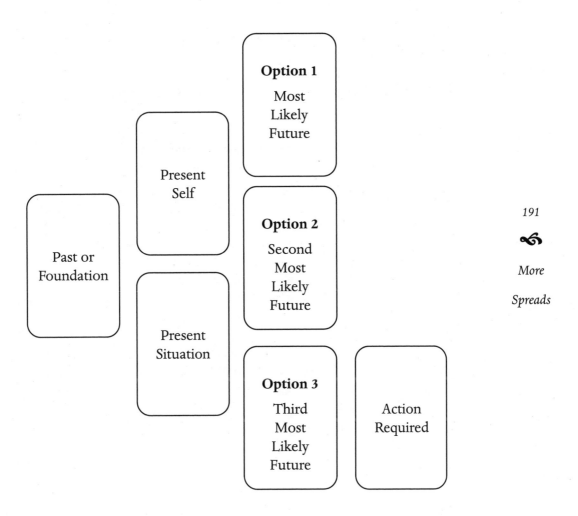

The Comparison Spread

The Choices Spread

If you have to make a choice from two or more options, this is a good spread to use. First place two cards representing the question and the querent's position in this situation. Then split the deck into as many parts as you have choices, and from each take one card to represent the outcome of that choice.

After studying each option and its outcome, using Gestalt techniques, draw an additional card for any choice where you are not clear as to the result. These clarification cards should provide greater insight. If there are any choices that still have unclear results, draw yet another card for each, up to three cards.

By this time you should have discovered the most favorable choice. If you were leaning toward one choice in the beginning, and the outcome is not looking good, don't keep drawing cards indefinitely until you get the answer you want.

What if all the choices seem to result in negative outcomes? Then consider the possibility that there are options you haven't thought of. Draw another card to stand for the first unknown, unconsidered option, and one or two more cards for clarification. If necessary, draw another card to represent a second unknown option and expand on that.

More options are usually available to us than we see at first. You might ask, "Should I buy that parcel of land?" Well, you could buy it, or you could leave it alone: two choices. Or you could lease it (third option), or lease with an option to buy (fourth option), or buy it with a partner (fifth option), or form a corporation to buy it (sixth option), or buy part of it (seventh option), or buy it and also the neighboring land (eighth option). Always assume there are more choices, and seek them out. (From Amber K's files, source unknown.)

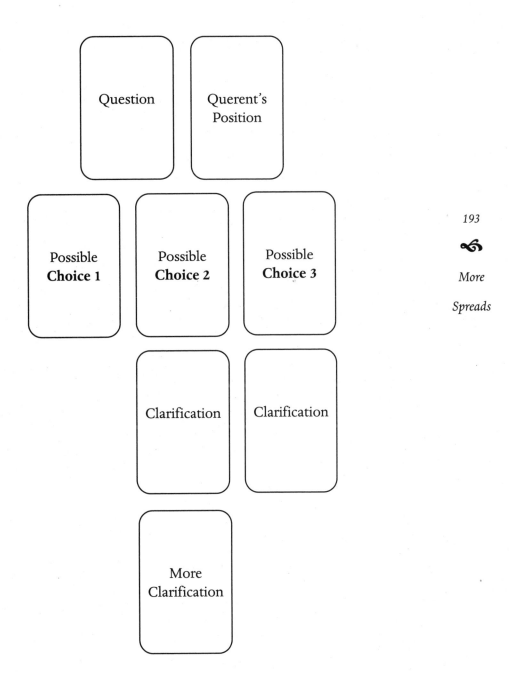
The Choices Spread

A Seven-Card Spread

Seven cards are dealt left to right. The first cards, on the left, represent the past; the middle three the present; and the two on the right, the future. Starting at the left, the card positions are as follows:

1. The Distant Past

2. The Immediate Past

3. Present Difficult Influences

4. You, As You Are Now

5. Present Positive Influences

6. Recommended Action

7. The Ultimate Result

This is adapted from a more traditional form, in which cards are read either right-side-up or reversed; the reversed or inverted cards show influences that are opposite in meaning, or at least weakened or delayed. If the querent asks a "yes-or-no" question and the majority of the cards are reversed, then the answer is "no."

However, when it is read Gestalt-style, all the cards can be placed and read upright. Of course the spread cannot then be forced to give a simple "yes" or "no" answer, but that is all right since most questions do not have such a black-or-white answer anyway.

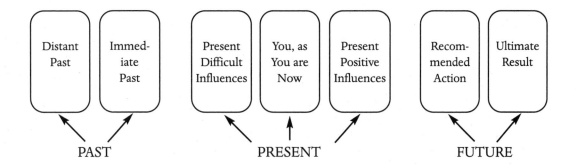

PAST   PRESENT   FUTURE

195

More

Spreads

The Yes–No Spread

In this quite common spread, you formulate your question, then lay out an odd number of cards. The premise here is that if most of the cards are right side up, the answer is "yes." If most of the cards are reversed, the answer is "no." The middle card, however, counts double: two yes or two no responses.

If there are an equal number of each, then you've got a "maybe." In theory this can happen if you're not concentrating, if you don't really want to know the answer, or if there are matters that will affect the answer but are not yet decided.

If you want more than a bald "yes" or "no," then you interpret the cards. The cards to left of center stand for the past, the center or "key" card is the present, and the right-hand cards represent the future.

Personally I do not recommend that you make life choices based simply on how many cards are reversed, but this spread can be useful in that it makes you think about the question in more depth than you might have otherwise.

Further, *your reaction* to the spread's recommendation (yes or no) can be extremely useful. Suppose you ask, "Should I take the job with Consolidated Wombat Engineering?" Four out of five cards are upright: the spread says "Yes." But your instant reaction is revulsion, and you start muttering, "Okay, that can't be right, best two out of three decides it."

Or perhaps the spread says "no," and your reaction is to yell at the cards, "Are you nuts? This is the best job opportunity I've ever had! No way am I going to turn it down!" In either case you have learned something about your gut reaction or instinctive response to the question. In a situation like this, learn from the cards in the spread, but listen to your instincts before you make a final decision.

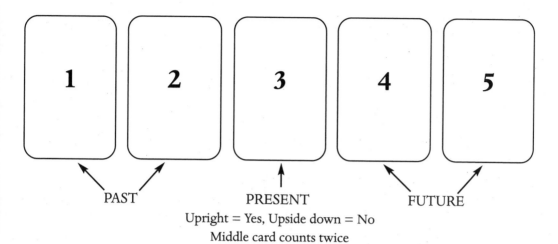

PAST · PRESENT · FUTURE

Upright = Yes, Upside down = No
Middle card counts twice

More

Spreads

Creating Your Own Spread

Sometimes none of the spreads shown here seem to apply to your specific situation or your querent's. Then it is perfectly all right to create your own spread.

Begin by brainstorming as many questions as you can regarding the situation. For example, Kimberly comes to you and says, "Richard is starting to get serious about our relationship, and I think he may ask me to marry him. I'm not sure how I feel or what I should say if he asks me."

What are some questions which might help her answer the larger question? If you brainstorm together, you might come up with a list like this:

- How do I see marriage (in general, not just with Richard)?
- How do I feel about getting married (in general)?
- What do I like best about Richard?
- What do I like least about Richard?
- What factor or factors would support the marriage and help it succeed?
- What factor or factors would hinder the marriage and perhaps destroy it?
- What do I want from marriage?
- What are the pros of getting married soon?
- What are the cons of getting married soon?
- What are the advantages to waiting a few years?
- What are the disadvantages to waiting a few years?
- What would the marriage be like financially (prosperity, possessions)?
- What would the marriage be like emotionally?
- What would the marriage be like as far as intellectual stimulation and companionship?
- What would the marriage be like as far as energy, success, and the accomplishment of my goals?
- What would the marriage be like as far as a spiritual bond, or spiritual growth?
- What would my relationship(s) with Richard's relatives be like?
- What best sums up the energies surrounding this possible marriage?

- What would this marriage be like as far as having and raising children?

- How would this marriage affect my career?

- If we got married, would we have fun together?

Once you have created a list of questions, refine it. You may add some questions, drop some, or change the wording. Then put them in some kind of logical order. After working with Kimberly's list, the questions looked like this:

1. What is my foundation for understanding marriage; how have I seen marriage practiced by my parents and others?

2. How do I see marriage now (in general, not just with Richard)?

3. How do I feel about getting married (in general)?

4. What do I want from marriage?

5. What factor or factors would support a marriage with Richard and help it succeed?

6. What factor or factors would hinder this marriage and perhaps destroy it?

7. What would this marriage be like financially (prosperity, possessions)?

8. What would this marriage be like emotionally?

9. What would this marriage be like as far as intellectual stimulation and companionship?

10. What would this marriage be like as far as energy, success, and the accomplishment of my goals?

11. What would this marriage be like as far as a spiritual bond or spiritual growth?

12. What would this marriage be like as far as having and raising children?

13. How would this marriage affect my career?

14. If we got married, would we have fun together?

15. What best sums up the energies surrounding the future of this marriage?

You can see that we dropped the questions about timing, so that we could just focus on learning whether the marriage would be a good thing. Asking "now or later" seems to imply that the marriage is a foregone conclusion, and might affect the rest of the reading. We can always do a separate reading on timing later, if Kimberly and Richard decide to get married.

The "what do I like or dislike about Richard" questions seemed silly to Kimberly; she had already thought a lot about those issues, and her journal was full of thoughts. She felt she already had a clear understanding of her likes and dislikes.

We also dropped the question about getting along with Richard's relatives, because Kimberly had thought about this as well. All his relations lived a long way away, they had little influence on his life, and anyway she had met them and they all liked her.

We did add two questions: one about Kimberly's view of marriage as she had seen it with her own parents, and one summing up the potential future of this marriage.

We are left with fifteen questions. That's a lot, but it's an important matter and needs to be explored in some depth. Does this mean we will have a fifteen-card spread? Not necessarily. Some questions may be easily answered with one card, but others are more complicated and might need additional cards. The simplest way to handle this is to start with fifteen cards, and if a given card seems obscure then we can draw more until we feel clear about the answer.

In what pattern shall we lay out the cards? This is a matter of personal preference. If your questions are on a timeline (past-present-future), then you can lay out the cards left to right, top to bottom, or whatever seems right to you. You can group them in any way that seems logical. Here's what we came up with for Kimberly's Spread:

Kimberly's Spread

The pattern is not important, as long as it makes sense to the querent and you can keep track of the questions and their positions.

The card positions can represent anything that is an important factor in the original question: individual people, events, potential options or choices, energies or influences, positive and negative factors, planetary spheres, and so on. Here is a partial list of factors or card positions that could be part of a spread:

- Myself at this moment (sometimes called the Significator)

- Other individuals (family members, partner or spouse, boyfriend or girlfriend, boss, etc.)

- Resources or help

- Blocks or obstacles

- Root, foundation or origin

- Power source or motivation

- Your feelings (or another's)

- Your thoughts (or another's)

- Your role (or another's)

- Your wants, desires, hopes (or another's)

- Your needs (or another's)

- Your fears (or another's)

- Relationship

- Necessary actions

- Advantages (this may be too general, so consider making it more specific)

  - Advantage to physical health

  - Advantages to family

  - Advantage to mental health, intellectual stimulation, etc.

- Disadvantages (ditto)

- Spiritual purpose

- Distant past or recent past

- Present influences (again, you may want to make it more specific)

  - Career influence

  - Family influence, etc.

  - Future influences (ditto)

  - Influence on family

  - Influence on career

  - Influence on finances, etc.

- Unknown factor

- Short-term future outcome

- Probable long-term outcome

- The key factor in the situation

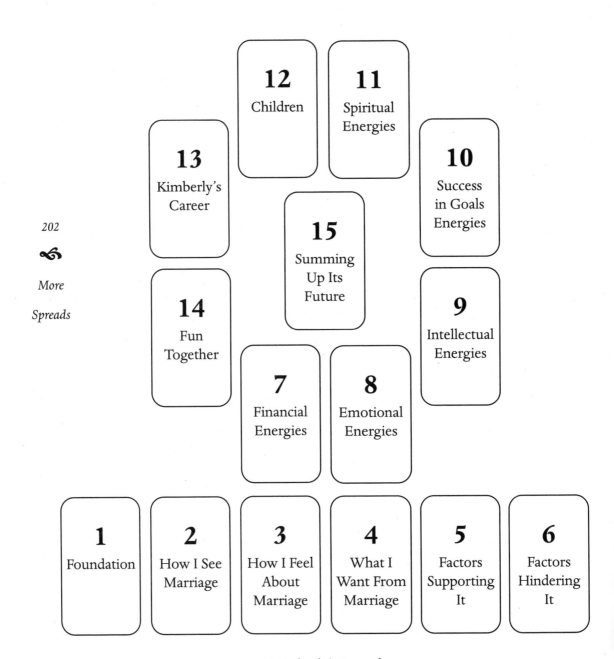

Kimberly's Spread
"What are the energies surrounding a marriage between Richard and me?"

Another example of a reading tailored to the question: you are having conflict in your family (or at work), and don't know what to do. Draw a card for the root of the problem, one for the role of each important person involved, one for the current situation, one for what is perpetuating the problem, and one suggesting the action you could take to alleviate the problem.

For a reading for a business situation, you may want a card representing your company's goal, one for your strategy, one for each of your top managers, one for each key department, one showing the company's greatest weakness, one symbolizing its greatest strength, one representing your customers (or each major client or group of customers), one representing recent market trends, and three representing your best moves to help the company succeed.

And so on. Creating your own spread is easy once you have done it a few times. It takes some thought about your question or situation, but doing that thinking and designing the spread may have you halfway to a solution before you even draw a card.

One more thing: in every situation, there is likely to be a person or factor having the power to change trends, confound probabilities, and create unexpected possibilities. In the traditional Gestalt Spread, this is represented by the Vesta card, the "Unknown Factor." You could just as well call it the Wild Card or the Coyote card (after the Southwestern trickster). Whatever you call it, it is wise to include a spot for it in any spread you design, just so you have an inkling of what could happen if. . . .

Chapter 11

The Professional Reader

Many people read Tarot only for their own guidance and insight, or occasionally without charge for friends and relatives. Others, such as priestesses and priests of Wicca, read Tarot as a form of pastoral counseling for those in their spiritual community. A rare few decide that reading the cards is their vocation, and seek to make it their livelihood. You may be one of these.

Your Motivation

Why do you want to read for a living? It is important that you be very clear about your motives before you quit your day job and take the plunge as a professional reader. Ask yourself these questions:

- Do I think it's easy money, or a good income without too much effort?

    It's not. To do it right takes a lot of energy and concentration during a reading, and at least as much work doing advertising and publicity, including free talks to promote Tarot and your services; plus accounting, study, and so on.

- Do I expect to receive status and admiration for my wonderful skills and insights?

    If you are reliably psychic and read Tarot using those skills, you can get a lot of ego strokes. Just always be right. If you use Gestalt Tarot to empower your clients, you may be appreciated but you probably won't be regarded with awe.

- Do I feel a strong connection with the Tarot and a deep desire to serve others using my skills?

    This is probably the only motivation that makes sense.

Do You Have the Skills?

More tough questions!

- Am I really, really skilled at reading the Tarot? Do I consistently have people asking for readings, and are they always pleased with the results?

- Do I have the stamina and concentration to do several readings a day without getting bored or losing focus?

- Can I do an excellent reading even if I am tired, or hungry, or in a bad mood?

- Do I like people a lot—almost any kind of people? Can I work with a wide variety of clients, from grouchy skeptics to desperate jilted lovers to helpless innocents who want a guru to guide their lives?

- Do I have enough wisdom, eloquence, and charisma to leave every client with a feeling of hope and determination, no matter how difficult their problems?

- Am I able to empower the client to find their own answers and make their own decisions, even if I am just *sure* I know what they should do in a given situation? Do I have the ability to sit on my own opinions and help them find their own path?

- Can I survive on a minimal income until my practice is established, and a modest but erratic income even if everything goes well?

    This is not for people who love the security of a regular paycheck, good medical benefits, and a company-supported pension plan. And unless you live in Hollywood and manage to become "Card Reader to the Stars," don't look for significant money.

- Do I have the skills of a business manager and a sales person, to handle advertising, promotion, and record-keeping, especially if I am working solo instead of with an established business?

Solo Practice or in Partnership?

Setting up your own business and being responsible for every aspect can be overwhelming for some people, especially those who do not have any knack for handling money or doing marketing. Many readers choose instead to associate themselves with a metaphysical, occult, New Age, or spiritual bookstore. In return for a percentage of the reader's fees, the store provides a quiet, private space for readings, as well as publicity in their mailings and other advertising.

This has some obvious advantages. The store is doing marketing and promotion anyway for their books and other merchandise, and perhaps for classes as well; it's not much trouble to publicize your Tarot readings along with everything else. It saves you the trouble and expense of launching your own marketing campaign. The store provides a safe, neutral, accessible location for readings; clients are sometimes reluctant to come to a private home for readings, even if they can find it easily. The regular customer traffic in the store provides a steady stream of potential clients who are already predisposed to be positive toward the Tarot, or at least open-minded. Conversely, people who come in for a reading tend to hang around and shop, so the store benefits. Some clients will like their reading so much that they will immediately buy Tarot decks and books from the shop.

If you are drawn to this kind of arrangement, visit the nearest such shop. Spend some time exploring the place before you approach the manager. See if it feels warm and inviting, and if the psychic and emotional energy is clear and positive. Notice whether there is room for a reader's nook, or possibly an attached classroom, meeting room, or office you could adapt for readings when nothing else is scheduled there. If everything feels right, then introduce yourself to the manager and make your proposal. Offer to do a complimentary reading for them, so they can judge the quality of your work. Have a written summary of your training and experience in Tarot, and possibly some client testimonials.

The manager may be sympathetic, but already have an arrangement with a reader. If that person is anything but a Tarot reader (an astrologer, palm reader, etc.), point out that adding Tarot will increase the customers' choices and draw new clients who are specifically interested in Tarot. If there is already a Tarot reader who is only present part-time, ask whether you could fill in during the open times or days.

It may be that you will be referred to an owner or another manager; be persistent until you talk to the person who has the authority to make a decision. If the response is favorable, offer to draft a written contract and to come in during a trial period (perhaps three months), and continue if everyone is happy.

Then treat this just as you would a job anywhere. If the shop advertises that readings will be available at certain times and days, come in consistently and on time. If readings are by appointment only, make sure you are very accessible: we're talking cell phone or pager with you at all times, an answering machine at home just in case, and prompt responses on your part.

If you decide to be at the store at regular hours, and no clients show up, then spend the time studying Tarot books or helping around the shop. Don't be too proud to help clean up or stock shelves or help create a new Tarot products display. Be friendly with the staff and communicate a lot with them, as long as you don't interfere with their work. This might even lead to a part-time position on the staff, if you want it.

If the shop sponsors classes and you are a good teacher (see chapter 13, "Teaching the Tarot"), you can supplement your readings by teaching Tarot classes evenings and weekends. Not only will you keep part of the class registration fees, but some of the students will come back for individual readings if they like your classes.

The Legal Context

People have been arrested for reading Tarot, not just in Europe during the Inquisition, but in the United States within the past few years. Some municipalities still have laws on the books against fortunetelling. Like many statutes left over from the past couple of centuries, they are routinely ignored by the police unless someone complains. However, it is best to be on the safe side and check your city, county, and state laws to see if you can get in trouble. If there is such a law still in effect, you may decide to redefine what you are doing (spiritual advisor?) or lobby to get the law changed. In the latter case, try not to attract the attention of certain religious types who hate anything smacking of the occult and love to legislate other people's behavior.

Be careful how you define yourself: if there are no laws against reading Tarot, then you can certainly advertise yourself as a Tarot reader. If you advertise as something else, you may run afoul of state laws requiring credentials and certification before you can use certain titles. For example, in most states you can be an advisor or personal counselor or pastoral counselor without having a degree or passing state boards; but you cannot necessarily advertise as a psychological counselor or therapist. Do check the laws in your state.

Zoning laws may prevent you from running a business out of your home if your neighborhood is zoned for strictly residential use. You might need to get special permission (a variance) from your local zoning board or planning commission before you can proceed. This might require notifying your neighbors of what you propose, and attending a public hearing. The alternative is to mention it to neighbors and hope they don't object, but if they do, you have a problem. If you do your readings at a bookstore, presumably it is in a commercial zone and there should be no difficulty.

If you are not operating under the umbrella of a store, you may need a business license from your city or county. These are not expensive or hard to obtain, but a license does put you into the system and you may have to pay local taxes on your income. Then there are state taxes, and the question of whether you want to incorporate as a proprietary business, a partnership, or a corporation. Find a local attorney who is savvy about business law—you can ask some local business owners who they recommend—and ask how you should set up your business to be legal.

All this is a far cry from the village wise woman days, when you just did your thing for the neighbors and they brought you the occasional chicken. If you are going to do this full-time today, however, it is important to cover all your legal bases. You do not want to be vulnerable if religious right-wingers launch a crusade against "Oh-kultism, Demon Worship, and Suchlike Threats," and decide that includes you and the local tea-leaf reader.

What Do Clients Want?

It is almost easier to say what clients *don't* want when they come for a Tarot reading. They don't want pretense or scams, or to be charged a shocking amount.

They often want guidance in making important life decisions. Some want to be told who they should marry, whether they should change jobs, or what investments to make. Others have already decided what they want to do, and simply want you to confirm that it's the right decision. But, as we have discussed, any time that you get into the business of running other people's lives, you take on a terrible responsibility. It's a no-win situation for the reader: either you make good decisions for them and they become dependent on your advice; or you make bad decisions and they blame you. So this is one need that you should not fulfill; always make it clear that the querent is responsible for their own life choices.

Some clients come for the ambience, the air of mystery, the thrill of watching as you Pierce the Veil of the Future on their behalf. They are there as much for entertainment as for information. While you should never compromise the quality of the reading, it does no harm to provide a little atmosphere and to play up the mystery. Candlelight, incense, soft music, and a little lecture about the ancient origins of the Tarot will set the mood. Then put a little extra drama in your voice and spice up the verbiage slightly: "It seems your life is at a crossroads, Linda. . . ." [Well, everyone's life is always at a crossroads.] "Have you the courage to see what lies ahead?" [Hope so, since that's what you're paying for].

Of course, it is easy to overdo this and come across as a total cornball. Be a little restrained; have fun, but no fake Transylvanian accents, please.

Setting Fees

The challenge is to charge a fair price for your time and skills, but not more than the market will bear. You may want to see what the competition is charging in your area. Are there psychic advisors, palm readers, or other Tarot readers in your town or city? Invest some money and go to a few; not only will you learn how much they charge and how long the sessions last, but you will get useful ideas on how to set up your own service. (Just as valuable will be the parts you don't like, and can be sure to avoid: clouds of choking incense, a cluttered or dirty room, an arrogant attitude ("Madame Zelda knows all, sees all"), irritating turns of phrase, or whatever.

When you are calculating your charges, remember that you may have expenses as well: a percentage to the bookstore where you read, advertising costs, business cards, commuting or set-up time, and so on. So don't undercharge, unless you do it intentionally in order to prime the pump until you have a regular clientele.

You will need to decide whether to charge a flat fee or by the hour. If you charge by the hour, about how long will an average reading take—and is there a cap or maximum fee? Will you take checks, cash, or credit cards?

Setting Your Hours

If you do readings at a bookstore, you might want to consult with the manager. Ask what the busiest times and days are; if people have time to come in and shop for books, they have time to get a Tarot reading. Be prepared to work some evening and weekend hours; more and more couples have two jobs, and the pool of housewives with time free on weekdays is shrinking.

Whatever hours you set, be sure to stick to them consistently and don't plan other activities at those times, even if business is slow. An erratic schedule will discourage clients. On the other side of the coin, you may need to be flexible and work at unusual times if that's when a client is available.

Do not overbook yourself. If your business thrives and lots of folks come in, you may be tempted to start scheduling back-to-back readings without a break in between. Don't. Make sure you get a break between readings, even if a client has to wait five minutes. Walk around, get some fresh air, have a light snack, drink some water, and clear your mind of the last reading so that you don't accidentally carry over ideas to the new one.

Publicizing Your Services

As mentioned earlier, if you have an arrangement with a metaphysical bookstore they may handle some publicity for you. However, don't rely completely on the store's efforts. Make sure there is a prominent, attractive sign in the store announcing your services and hours. Help them write copy for their newsletter, mailings, and ads, and arrange a good display of Tarot books and merchandise with another little sign about you.

Get business cards printed. A local printer can help you choose from standard designs and colors, or design something unique for an extra charge. Possibly you have an artistic friend who could help you design a logo. Once you have the cards, spread them everywhere; make sure they are posted at local supermarkets, laundromats, hairstyling salons, and anyplace else with a bulletin board or literature rack.

Most importantly, arrange to speak at local clubs and organizations. Sometimes service clubs that meet weekly need entertaining and informative presentations. You may not get paid for your talk, but you can hand out cards and let people know about your services. You may also be able to wangle an invitation to interview on a local radio show.

If you are not a great public speaker, find a friend who is and get them to coach you as you create and practice your presentation, or join a group like Toastmasters. The first few times are the hardest. In time, you will find yourself relaxing and enjoying yourself. Include some history of the Tarot, explain how it can be helpful, and tell a couple of stories (without names) or interesting or humorous experiences you have had while reading the Tarot. Also try to get some visual aids, such as slides, viewgraphs, or enlarged posters of the Major Arcana (which you can make at a photocopy shop).

A note here about copyright: Most publishers allow copying of small sections of a book, or pictures, as long as the copies are going to be used for educational purposes only, not sold. Do credit the author and publisher so your students can get their own originals. Read the copyright notice in the front of the book, and please play by the publisher's rules. Those of us who make our living creating copyrighted material thank you.

Your Agreement with the Client

Once the client is comfortable, but before the reading begins, make sure the terms of the reading are clear. Few things are more embarrassing than to finish a reading and then discover that the client thought it was a free service from the bookstore, or done by voluntary donation, or whatever. You can say something like, "Let me just review how this works. I've set aside one hour for our reading, and the fee will be $50. If it does take a bit longer, there's no extra charge. We can take care of that at the end of the reading; cash or check is fine, or you can put it on your credit card at the front of the shop. Do you have any questions about that part of it?"

Once in a rare while the client may ask, "Is the reading guaranteed?" What they are asking is whether they can get their money back if your predictions don't come to pass. This is a chance for you to explain that you are not doing prophecy, that everyone involved has free will and can change the expected outcome at any time, and add, "If you are not satisfied with the reading for any reason, there's no charge." In other words, "Satisfaction guaranteed"; and if you are a competent reader, chances are you'll never be asked for a refund.

If the client balks at the fee, give them choices. For example, "If you would prefer, I can do a reading in half an hour for $30. It will be a little more general, but we can still cover the essentials of your question." If the client likes that idea, then use the Condensed Spread. But always give the client options; that's just good customer service.

The Environment

As discussed in chapter 7, you will want a space that is quiet, private, clean, and attractive, whether you do your readings at a bookstore or at home.

If you are reading in a bookstore's office or classroom, or even on the main merchandise floor, you may not have the freedom to create the space exactly as you would like. It may be possible at least to set up a tall partition, possibly covered with an interesting print fabric, as a way of gaining the illusion of privacy, reducing an over-large space, or blocking an unattractive view.

Preparing Yourself Mentally

You will know you are not in a proper frame of mind to read Tarot if you are feeling agitated, vulnerable, unbalanced, flighty, or distracted.

When you greet a client you should be grounded, centered, and focused. Grounding is connecting with Earth energies so that you feel stable, solid, and strong. Centering means placing your consciousness at the center of your being and identity. Focusing is putting all your attention on one person, thing, process, or experience. There is some overlap in all these terms; if you have achieved one of these states you are on your way to achieving the others.

Even if you think you are feeling ready, it is helpful to do some simple exercises before the reading. You may discover some vestiges of tension or distraction that you weren't even consciously aware of.

You can ground yourself by sitting quietly and sending an energy cord from your root chakra, at the base of your spine, deep into the Earth. Allow any jitters or weakness to flow down and out of you through the cord, and then draw up strength. Another way to ground is to lie full length on the Earth (grass is nice), and let the same kind of energy exchange happen. You may be able to ground through your hands, by holding a fairly large rock and letting any tension flow into it. A smooth, rounded river stone somewhere between the size of an egg and a cantaloupe is good. Some readers wear a necklace or amulet of hematite, pyrite, or other heavy gemstone if they have trouble staying grounded. Last but not least, food has a grounding effect, which is one reason that many rituals include cakes and wine or other food toward the end. Don't stuff yourself before a reading, and don't eat sugar or other stimulants; but a protein snack like cheese or meat can help.

To center, imagine a large house with many rooms. The house represents your life, and the rooms represent different aspects of your life: your work, your home, friends, hobbies, organizations you belong to, memories, fantasies, and so on. Begin at the front door and move through the rooms and hallways until you come to the room at the very center; this is your haven, the place which holds the essence of you. It may look like a favorite place from your childhood, or your present bedroom, or a simple room with an altar in the center. If it contains a mirror, it will show you as you feel inside, not as you look to the outside world. It will feel absolutely safe and secure. Just be in this room for a little while, and you will become centered emotionally.

Focusing involves the release of all worries, distractions, and even awareness of anything outside the focal point. Some readers use a form of *raja yoga* meditation; for example, concentrating on a candle flame or faceted gemstone until the rest of the world disappears. Listening to music may help, or floating in a warm bath. You can also learn the arts of *pranayama*, or yogic breathing. An exercise called *bhramari* breathing helps concentration: inhale deeply through your nose, then hum in a long, slow exhalation. Do it again, and make the tone more even and the exhalation longer. Keep doing this for several breaths, and you will feel very calm, still, and focused.

There may be times that these techniques are not enough to put you in the right frame of mind. If a reading appointment is approaching and you know you cannot give your best, consider calling the client and rescheduling for a later date. Then focus on your own emotional and spiritual needs.

On The Telephone

No, this is not about ordinary telephone etiquette. Some clients may occasionally want Tarot readings over the telephone, especially loyal clients who move to another area. Gestalt Tarot can be done this way, most easily if you and the querent have identical decks and a speakerphone. As the querent turns the cards over, they will tell you what the card is, and you can rapidly find the card in your deck and place it in the corresponding position in front of you.

Make the appointment in advance and have the querent call you for the reading; this saves you the trouble of billing for the phone charges as well as your services.

The telephone is probably not the ideal medium for human interaction, since the nuances of body language and eye contact are not available, at least until picture phones become more common. However, it is better than interaction via computer, since at least you can hear the client's tone of voice.

Dress and Grooming

How should you dress as a professional reader? Some readers like to play up the drama, and wind up looking like stereotyped Gypsy fortunetellers or stage magicians. Such costumes are colorful but can provoke skepticism in your clients.

Other readers go to the opposite extreme, wearing ordinary business clothes. This can promote the feeling in your clients that they have come in to have their taxes prepared or to discuss mutual funds. The mystery of the Tarot is lost entirely.

There is a third choice, which is to dress in normal, semi-casual clothing (such as a blouse or turtleneck and slacks), but with a striking piece of jewelry to mark the occasion as something special. I sometimes wear all black with an amber necklace and earrings. A pendant necklace with an interesting talisman can be intriguing. This sort of ensemble has the advantage that it looks special, but not so complicated or colorful that the client is distracted from the reading.

Welcoming Your Client

When your client first arrives, make them feel welcome by standing and moving to greet them. Offer your hand, make eye contact, and smile. Make some comment such as, "Ms. Boniface? I'm Joan Pyewacket. I'm so glad to meet you." Invite the client in, take their coat if they have one, and show them where to sit. Then it's a good idea to offer them tea or coffee, and spend a couple of minutes chatting before you get down to business. You can get the conversation going by asking where they heard about you, whether they have previous experience with Tarot readings, or the usual chit-chat: "Are you a native of (this city)?" "Incredible weather we're having, isn't it?" "Have you visited *The Metaphysical Maven* (this store) before?"

Pay attention to the client's voice and mannerisms. If they are nervous about having a Tarot reading, it will show up right away in the tense way they hold themselves, a tight and slightly higher-pitched voice, lack of eye contact, fidgeting, or other signs. A nervous client will need some extra time to relax. After the first few minutes of conversation, you can casually mention that, "Some of my clients are a little nervous about their first reading. That's very natural, since they don't understand the process and are talking to a stranger. I hope you don't find me intimidating." This gives the client an opening for a disclaimer and a chance to talk about their fears at the same time: "Oh no, it's not you, it's just that I've never done this before. . . ."

More Customer Service

Thinking in terms of customer service will help your reading business thrive. It is all the more important because you are not selling a material product for the client to carry home, use, and enjoy. If someone buys the fishing pole they want and the price is fair, they will put up with ho-hum service from the sales clerk. You're not selling fishing poles, you're selling an experience that includes human interaction, mental stimulation and insight, and a little entertainment.

Customer service includes several things:

- Promptness (be on time for readings, and finish when you said you would)

- Friendliness (smile, it won't hurt your face)

- Dress and grooming (clean, neat clothing, nice hair, fresh breath, etc.)

- Consistency (in price and the entire experience)

- Knowledge (of your field, Tarot)

- Communications (eye contact, body language, tone of voice, choice of words, and active listening skills)

- Environment (clean, attractive, and as private as possible)

- Courtesy ("please," "thank-you," "Mister" or "Ms" unless they've specifically asked you to call them by their first name, and so on)

- Respect (never talk down to the client; and treat all ages, races, religions, genders, and ethnic groups with the same courtesy and service)

Last but not least, ask the client if there's anything else they need to make them comfortable at the beginning or to help them understand the reading at the end.

The Reading

The process of the reading is discussed in chapter 7. If you are reading for money, however, there is an additional factor to remember: timing.

First, time is valuable. If you are charging a set fee for a set time period, do not let the reading run on well past the time allotted. If new issues come up during a reading, or the question proves unexpectedly complex, then talk with the client about setting up another appointment to continue.

Because you are operating within a limited time span, you will have to keep the pace up and not get stuck in a long interpretation of one card. If, for example, you are using the standard Gestalt Spread (twelve cards) and doing one-hour readings, you will have about eight minutes for preliminaries, three and a half minutes for each of the twelve cards, and ten minutes to discuss the patterns, sum up, and reach closure. In other words, the client had better be turning over their seventh card at the half-hour mark, or you're running late. Keeping to a timeline is not the most enjoyable way to read Tarot, but it is a discipline you must acquire if you are going to read professionally.

Occasionally clients will ask if they can tape-record the reading, or even photograph the final spread. Fine, if the equipment works; occasionally the energies used during the event seem to interfere with such devices. Or they may want to make notes during the reading; but if the client is industriously writing everything throughout the reading it tends to lengthen it quite a bit. It is probably better to let the querent write notes only at the end, during the recap and summary.

Closure

At the close of the reading, you may want to provide a printed copy of the spread and let the querent note which cards came up where, so they can re-create the spread at home and study it further. Not all clients will want to do this, but it's a nice option to have available.

Occasionally a client gets so excited about their discoveries that they want to continue immediately with another reading on a separate issue. That may be possible if you don't have another appointment; but consider carefully whether you are fresh enough to go on, or whether you need to rest now and schedule another visit.

When the client gives you your fee, thank them and shake hands. There is a point to this apart from general friendliness. Studies have shown that touching or other kinesthetic input makes the entire experience more vivid and memorable. The smell of incense, the taste of coffee, and handling the cards all contribute to this effect, so don't let the reading be only a visual and auditory experience.

Be sure to give the client your card so that they can contact you again in the future. Wish them well, and walk them to the door (if in your home; it's not necessary in a shop, since they may decide to browse after the reading). Thank them and express your hope to see them again. Then take a break and rest.

Conclusion

Professional reading is not for everyone, and should not even be attempted unless you have another source of income (at least while you are getting started) and are willing to work hard at promoting your services as well as actually reading. You must also love the Tarot and enjoy people, even when they are talking about their problems. But given all this, professional Tarot reading can be a rewarding career. Good luck!

Chapter 12

Querents Who Present Special Challenges

Whether you are reading professionally or just occasionally for fun, you will find that most clients or querents are cooperative sorts of people who are quite willing to follow your lead to the best of their varying abilities. But every so often you will encounter one of those challenging individuals who remind us all that our primate ancestors emerged from the trees far too early. Your challenge is to deal with these special people in a mature, constructive, compassionate manner, and not to follow your first impulse to throttle them and bury them behind your zucchini plants. Here are some examples.

The Skeptic

"This is all baloney, anyway."

The Skeptic will inform you, with a scowl (if he was pressured into coming by his girlfriend) or a smirk (if she came under her own power) that she doesn't really "believe all this mumbo-jumbo" but only agreed to a reading for some perfectly logical reason, such as (choose one):

- My wife / girlfriend / boyfriend / dog made me do it"

- "I have to do a paper for my class on history / anthropology / psychology / English"

- "I was just curious (and I'm going to expose you as the devil-worshipping swine you are, you occult-dabbling, non-Bible-based, doomed-for-eternity pond scum)"

I recommend that you candidly discuss the client's doubts before you actually begin a reading. Explain that Gestalt Tarot is a cooperative endeavor, and if they are not willing to suspend their doubts and give it a fair effort, then there's no point in continuing. If they are completely close-minded, you can decline to proceed and save yourself time and frustration.

If the client agrees to try, they may gradually become open to the process when they discover that you are not going to do a Hollywood gypsy-fortune-teller number on them ("I see romance in your future . . . but the vision is fading . . . cross my palm with more silver and I shall try to pierce the veil. . . .").

Whatever your internal reaction, or your decision about proceeding, remain calm and professional or you will only confirm the client's worst imaginings.

220

Querents

Who

Present

Special

Challenges

The Monosyllabic Response

"Yes. No. I don't know."

Some people are naturally quiet, others may be nervous at their first Tarot reading, and a few utterly lack imagination. Any of them may answer every question with the fewest sounds a human can utter and still be classified as an intelligent life form.

The nervous ones will probably open up as they discover that you are warm and friendly and don't bite. You may need to spend some time making small talk, until you discover an interest that diverts them from self-consciousness. One of the all-time best icebreakers is to get someone talking about their pets, and then tell a funny story about your own dog/cat/iguana/whatever. Unless the querent's beloved Muffin died last week, it always works.

For the quiet ones, remember to ask open-ended questions, and then be silent long enough to show them that you are serious about expecting a response. Never let your impatience lead you to dive in and fill the silences, or the quiet querent will happily settle back and let you do all the talking—which, of course, makes Gestalt Tarot impossible.

A few people really do lack imagination. When you ask "What is the person on the throne thinking right now?" they will look at you as though you are on parole from the Institute for Those Who Believe They Are Bedspreads and retort, "It's just a picture, it's not thinking anything," or, "How the hell should I know?"

A technique used in Neuro-Linguistic Programming is very helpful with the "I don't know" answer. You'll be surprised at how many people will open up if you respond with, "But if you did know, what would it be?" And they'll probably never even notice that you just did an end run around them.

You cannot provide someone with a rich fantasy life on demand, or even a B-grade imaginative experience. You can minimize the storytelling aspect of Gestalt and go straight for the jugular: "Does that king remind you of anyone you know? Big guy with a beard? Charlie McMurtle? What's he like?" Relate the images to real-life figures and situations in the querent's life as quickly as possible, and let the reading be short. Remember that the point is to help the querent stand back and look at their own life, so they can make practical decisions.

The Talking-Head Analyst

"The Emperor represents my father, and in early childhood . . ."

A few clients love self-psychoanalysis, or the appearance of it. They can glance at a Tarot card and then rattle on for an hour about their own personality disorders, neuroses, and the origins of every mental nuance that flashes across their brain. They are so glib and verbose that you, the reader, may start glancing at your watch and wondering why you bothered to come.

The difficulty with such people is that, for some of them, it's all an intellectual game. Their insights into their thought processes may or may not be accurate, but their behavior doesn't change. Analysis does not lead to action, but replaces it. You may get the impression that they are gratified by their own sensitivity, impressed by their incisive understanding of themselves, almost in awe of their own brilliant grasp of everything that makes them tick. And there it ends.

Listening to such a client at a reading is a little embarrassing; it's like being hired to guide someone through the Everglades, then discovering that they just want you to sit on the edge of the swamp and watch them.

You have a few options in this situation. You can sit by the swamp, mentally compose your grocery shopping list while the querent plays games, then collect your fee. The client may be very happy at the "good work we've done here today," or they may be oddly disappointed that nothing real happened.

Or you can play tough cop and stop the client short every time they go into a canned monologue. You can ask harder and harder questions: "If you know you're failing in order to spite your domineering father, why don't you do something about it?" You can make it clear that clever analysis of the problem is never

221

Querents

Who

Present

Special

Challenges

enough; a responsible adult acts on their knowledge. Of course, the client may get mad and leave; or they may get serious and do some work.

You can also get subtle; ask your question, listen to the party line, and then ignore that response and ask again: "What *else* might the figure in the card be feeling?" Never buy the first reply; force the client to look deeper, but don't challenge them directly.

The Guru Seeker

"Grant me your wisdom, O great Tarot Master!"

222

Querents

Who

Present

Special

Challenges

How's your ego? If it's large enough, you may enjoy the client who wants to be your adoring acolyte. This person is looking for a parent/teacher stand-in who will be a lot more wise, loving, and charismatic than the genuine articles. The querent will hang on every drop of wisdom that falls from your lips, extol your virtues to everyone they meet, and spend more and more time around you. They will give you little gifts constantly, or expensive ones they can't afford. Unless you are an egomaniac, they will drive you nuts.

In response, you will modestly deny your godhood, and gently try to redirect their attention to their own strengths and inner resources. You will carefully explain the virtues of independence and self-trust, while they watch you like a hungry puppy, nod solemnly, agree totally, and ignore every word.

If it goes on long enough, they will become upset that you're not reading the script properly. Then they will discover some terrible flaw in you that shatters their faith. They will denounce you to all the same people to whom they nominated you for sainthood last week. They will disappear. Rather than risk this ever happening again, you will want to go live in a cave; but you won't do it, because your real puppy would miss you.

You can avoid some of the grief by putting a stop to the drama the minute you realize what's happening. Be direct, brusque, verbally brutal if necessary. Tell them you don't want to see them again. Do it, or resign yourself to playing the lead in their fantasy.

The Dependent Client

"I would never dream of making a move without asking . . ."

Some individuals are terrified at the thought of making a decision. They may have no sense of direction, no career goals, no mission in life. Or perhaps they have never developed the skills ancillary to decision-making, such as defining a problem, gathering information, setting standards, or doing comparison and analysis. Some simply have no faith in their own intuition, perhaps because they have made decisions in the past that turned out disastrously. Some do not believe, in their hearts, that mistakes can be remedied; therefore they are frightened of ever making one at all.

For all such people, the idea of a wise Tarot reader with special divinatory skills is wonderfully attractive. They may see you as a safe guide through the vicissitudes of life—a professional decision-maker who can relieve them of the intolerable burden of making their own choices. Or, it may be a particular choice they cannot make. They may be obsessing on one question, endlessly exploring every facet and nuance of the problem, and returning to you for readings over and over, even after the message of the Tarot is clear.

Of course, everyone can use help making decisions sometimes. Querents may be too close to a situation to understand it clearly, or may see it in a distorted way because of their prejudices and past experiences. They may lack information or experience important to a particular choice. So, every intelligent human occasionally seeks guidance from others, depending on the nature of the question and the kind of resources needed. One time they ask a friend, another time a professional mechanic, another time a priestess or priest.

The key here is that most adults ask for help occasionally, not every time they have to make a decision greater than mushroom-soup-or-tomato-for-lunch. Also, we seek help from a variety of sources, rather than becoming dependent on one counselor.

If you find yourself seeing the same client week in and week out for every type of life decision, or for a nagging problem they refuse to solve, what can you do? An unscrupulous reader would sit back and take the fees, allowing the querent's dependency or paralysis to line their pocket. A wiser and more ethical course of action is to help the querent look squarely at the issue, even if you have to offer a free reading on this topic: "What are the energies surrounding my dependence on (your name) for making so many decisions?"

Or, if it's the same question every time: "What is the impact on my life when I let this issue drag on, and refuse to settle it?"

Regardless of the client's reaction when you bring it up, remember that you are not the client's parent, nor should you become the enabler of their dependence and indecision. If necessary, you can always refuse to see them more than once a month, or refuse to revisit a nagging topic once it has been explored to the point of nausea (yours).

223

Querents

Who

Present

Special

Challenges

The Passive Client

"I'm paying for this; entertain me."

Some clients confuse Tarot reading with fortunetelling and arrive with the notion that you will simply peer at the cards and tell them their future while they nod silently. They will also be secretly expecting occult drama, and hoping you live in a brightly painted Gypsy wagon. You will need to explain the facts of Gestalt Tarot:

1. You are not a seer, with an uncanny ability to know the future.

2. You are not a psychic with the ability to read the querent's mind. The querent, who lives inside their head, is in a much better position to read their own mind.

3. You are not a channel for disembodied spirits who mysteriously happen to know more about the querent's life than the querent does.

4. Your job is to help the querent as a guide, facilitator, and asker of myriad questions.

5. The querent's job is to answer the questions using all the imagination at their disposal. The information gained in a Gestalt reading comes from the querent's own mind. Therefore, it works if the querent works.

The occasional client may be seriously disappointed that you cannot provide all the answers through some supernatural agency. If you lack a Romany accent and big hoop earrings, you have only compounded the situation. The least you can do is light some incense and throw on some dramatic costume jewelry.

224

Querents

Who

Present

Special

Challenges

The Deadbeat

"That wasn't what I expected. I'm not paying . . ."

If you are doing readings for a fee, it can be upsetting when a client refuses to pay, for whatever reason. It rarely happens, but it is wise to have a plan in case it does.

Sometimes you can avoid the problem just by explaining clearly up front what it is that you do and how much you charge. Then clients won't be disappointed in their expectations.

Then there is the client who promises payment that never arrives, sends a check that is only one-quarter the agreed-on fee, or simply gives you a rubber check. You can report it to the police, who may handle it very professionally, or may exhibit a certain lack of sympathy because they are thinking that one con artist (the client) bilked another (you).

My approach is to try contacting them once to request payment, and then to drop it. Spending more time and emotional energy than that wastes my resources for a very iffy chance of forcing payment. Besides, I have a strong belief in karma and the Law of Return, and know that the deadbeat will receive justice from other Hands than mine.

Needless to say I would not read for that individual again, or anyone referred by them.

The New Age Child of Light

"I love it when those cards with rainbows come up."

225

&

Querents

Who

Present

Special

Challenges

Very rarely you may meet a client who seems to be a late 1960s flower child, transported through time intact. They may be slightly repackaged for the new millennium, but the spirit is there. This client lives in a world of white light, healing crystals, guardian angels, positive spirits, rainbows, unicorns, and pretty, boring music made with instruments no one in North America has ever heard of.

The child of light interprets everything on a cosmic plane that is composed of fluffy clouds tinged with pastel colors. The chief problem with reading for them is that some have difficulty facing their shadow sides or admitting their own pain, fear, or anger. Nothing is wrong that can't be fixed with a little meditation, acupuncture, a new positive affirmation, and quartz crystal therapy; all of which are good, but the child of light sometimes looks for an external quick fix instead of the tough internal work that growing up requires.

All in all, such clients are rather lovable. You are not their therapist, so don't try to change them. You are allowed to remind them that they are responsible for their lives and perhaps to shine a little white light on the parts of their lives where they've forgotten that.

The Doomsayer

"I hate it when those cards with rainbows come up."

Some clients expect the worst and see it in every card. They make Eeyore (the gloomy donkey in *Winnie-the-Pooh*) look like the captain of the cheerleading squad. A cheery Tarot figure lifting a goblet is probably drinking himself to death. A victorious soldier has probably just come from a battlefield where half his men were slaughtered. A child holding flowers is either allergic or about to discover a bee the hard way.

You cannot change this person's outlook on life in the course of a Tarot reading. You cannot argue with their interpretations; chances are they are adept at the self-fulfilling prophecy, and if they see terrible things in a Tarot spread, those things (or something equally bad) may well happen, because the client will expect it and will unconsciously engineer it if possible.

You can, with some effort, help such clients to explore what effect their attitudes and actions have on their lives, and the possibility that the client might influence a more positive outcome.

226

Querents

Who

Present

Special

Challenges

The Tarot Expert

"An alternative interpretation based on the sixteenth-century Verbena-Bergamot deck would suggest . . ."

Some people know too much about Tarot. May you never have one as a client.

Gestalt Tarot works best with the fresh, innocent eyes of a client who does not know all the possible permutations of The Hierophant in twelve languages and on four continents. In Gestalt at its best, each card has an intensely personal meaning. For someone new to Tarot, the cards can be a pristine mirror reflecting their hopes, fears, modus operandi, and life choices. Knowing too many other people's interpretations simply clouds the mirror.

If your client starts sounding like a Tarot scholar, do your best to bring them to the present moment and offer them the gift of looking at the cards with fresh eyes ("Pretend you've never seen this image before . . .") If that proves impossible, then let them proceed to do their own reading based on their voluminous research, shut up, and accept your fee graciously at the end.

The Scaredy Cat

"Is this, like, spiritually dangerous?"

A client may be simultaneously intrigued by Tarot and afraid of it. Or they may be purely afraid, but have been bullied by one of your other loyal (and over-enthusiastic) clients into having a reading done.

Watch the eyes. If your client says little and looks like a deer trapped in the headlights, that's a bad sign. If your client's eyes dodge frantically around the room as though seeking the EXIT sign, that's also bad. These may be clients who are secretly sure that you are messing with occult forces forbidden to man.

Some pleasant chit-chat may eventually relax them enough to reveal their concerns. Make it clear that you have no pact with the Evil One, and emphasize the mundane psychological side of Tarot and its value in counseling and decision-making. If the client gets intrigued and wants to proceed, fine. If they don't relax, then you'll both probably be happiest if you sigh inwardly, suggest that this isn't something they really want to do, and let them off the hook.

The Naysayer

"I suppose that next you're going to say the sky is blue . . ."

227

Querents

Who

Present

Special

Challenges

Some people are just plain contrary. A skeptic is one thing, but an argumentative client who just likes a good scrap is even more difficult. If you try to do a traditional reading or a psychic reading, they will verbally eat you for lunch.

Fortunately, Gestalt Tarot is pretty much impervious to their style because you are asking questions and they are coming up with all the significant stuff. They can either argue with themselves, or fall back to a position of "That's a stupid question!" when you speak. To which you reply, "All right, what would be a better question?"—and then have them answer their own version.

If it gets too intolerable, you can always politely explain to the client that a minimal amount of cooperation would help the process along.

The Omen Watcher

"Oh God, not the Death card! I don't want to die!"

A few clients know just enough about Tarot to know that there are bad cards mixed in with the brave knights and happy peasants, but not enough to realize that the cards cannot always be taken literally.

An example is the client who freaks at the Death card. The Devil and the Tower are a distant second and third for panic purposes.

Here is is your chance to educate a client. Explain that the cards are symbolic, that Death usually refers to drastic change, or the death of an old habit or lifestyle, and that that can be a very positive thing. If necessary tell the client that you will draw a Clarifying Card to explore what the Death card refers to, which will dilute the impact and draw attention away from the grisly skeleton. Pray that you don't draw the Ten of Swords.

These kinds of clients are the exception. Most who come to you will be cooperative and appreciative of your efforts. In fact, you may finish each reading with a natural high from the elegance of the spread, the enthusiasm of the querent, and the satisfaction of helping another person deal with important questions. Remember these experiences on the rare occasion that you encounter the challenges.

Querents

Who

Present

Special

Challenges

Chapter 13

Teaching the Tarot

The best way to learn the Tarot is to teach it. It's amazing how motivated you can get when there's a class scheduled tonight and you're the instructor. All those people are counting on you to teach them some wonderful stuff, and you certainly don't want to disappoint them or embarrass yourself—so you study like a mad person to make sure it's a great class.

If you are a member of a Wiccan coven or another kind of metaphysical group, you have a ready-made student body just waiting to learn something as exciting and fascinating as Tarot. If you want to teach but aren't part of a group, you can rent a room and advertise your classes to the public. If you are not very experienced, you may not feel confident about advertising yourself as a Tarot instructor; in that case list yourself as a facilitator or discussion leader, and explain at the first class that you are still learning but want to share the experience with a group.

You may live in a community with an evening or weekend adult continuing education program, sponsored by a local college or school district. You can talk to the coordinator of the program and see if they would like to have a Tarot class. If so, not only will they handle basic publicity, but you can get paid for teaching. Do take your proposed class outline in when you talk to the head of the program.

However you arrange it, count on having fun and learning a lot when you teach. Here are several exercises you can use in teaching Tarot, as well as some class outlines incorporating them. In all of these exercises, remind yourself and your students to view the cards with fresh eyes, to respond to what they *see* in the cards, not to what they may *know* are the traditional meanings.

Exploring Different Decks

Have each student bring a different deck to class, or two or three if they have them. If some of your students don't have their own decks yet, you can bring several of your own and give each student time to look though one deck.

Then ask each student to speak about their deck, explaining why they like or don't like it, how it differs from the standard (using the *Rider-Waite* deck as standard is the easiest approach), and what they consider to be its strengths and weaknesses for reading. Then each student should pass their deck around the group, so every student can look at it more closely. Occasionally, you may have a student who doesn't want anyone else to handle THEIR cards, in which case, you can ask if they'd be willing to lay their cards out on a table to be viewed, with no touching.

As you finish passing each deck around, set it in the middle of the table or floor. By the end of the class, everyone should be a little more familiar with several decks new to them, and will probably be eager to get to the local metaphysical bookstore and buy that deck they fell in love with.

You might consider talking to the manager of the bookstore about a discount for your students. Explain that you are teaching Tarot and that you would be happy to send your students to this shop to purchase decks, but could they have, say, ten percent off the retail price? If the manager agrees, get a coupon or discount certificate for each of your students and distribute them at the end of the first class.

Gestalt Tarot Get-Acquainted Exercise

Each student selects three cards from their own deck which they feel describe them. Going round robin, each person shows their cards and explains why each is appropriate. If you wish, you can structure it so that you ask each student to pick:

- The card that best represents you

- The card that represents your job or vocation

- The card that represents your hopes and dreams for the future

For example: "My name is Suzanne, and I chose the Queen of Cups to represent me, because I love the ocean and also because I think love is the most important thing in life, and the Queen symbolizes that for me. I chose the Five of Pentacles for my job, because I'm a registered nurse and the card shows a woman comforting an injured man. And I chose the Four of Wands for my hopes and dreams, because I want to own my own home someday and this castle looks like a very safe and snug home to me."

Comparing Deck Imagery

With several decks on hand, pick out the same trump from each—for example, the Fool—and place them in the center of the group. Then compare the design, colors, images, and symbolism in depth. Sometimes you will find that the layers of meaning in a given card become clearer when you see several different artists' interpretation of the same theme.

Exploring One Card in Depth Using Gestalt Techniques

Get several color copies of the same card. Ask each student to move to a different part of the room and meditate on the card. Some things they may consider:

- What is the first thing you notice about the card?

- What is the overall feeling you get from the card?

- What are the dominant colors in the card? What do you feel when you see those colors?

- How would you describe the character of the main figure in the card?

- What are some of the most striking objects or symbols in the card?

- What are some possible meanings of the card?

- How does this card apply to your life?

After each person has had at least ten minutes to study the card, come back together as a group and share your impressions and ideas.

Games with Tarot

Many common card games can be played with a Tarot deck, although you may have to use only the Minor Arcana. For example, they can be adapted to "Go Fish," "Old Maid," and solitaire. This is a light and amusing way to help students become more familiar with the cards. Give them homework to play solitaire or another card game with the cards.

Tarot Haiku Poems

Haiku is a traditional Japanese form of poetry. Each poem consists of three lines, with a total of seventeen syllables or fewer. Usually haiku uses concrete images to convey meaning, and "records the essence of a moment keenly perceived in which nature is linked with human nature" (Cor van den Heuverl, editor of *The Haiku Anthology*). Because the poems are so short, the poet must capture the meaning, feeling, image, or impression in as vivid and concise a way as possible.

This form lends itself well to teaching Tarot, because it makes students think about the core meaning or essence of each card. Have each student choose a card, deliberately or at random, and write a haiku about it. Then share and discuss your haiku, and do it again with new cards.

As an alternative, have each student write a haiku about every card in the Major Arcana. It will take a few classes to get through them all! Then it might be fun to choose the best haiku for each trump, and "publish" the whole collection for them to keep. (Make sure each student gets at least one poem in the final collection, so no one feels left out.)

Here are some examples of haiku based on the Fool card.

> Bright sun above
> Broken death below
> Happy wanderer in between

> Strolling
> Among dangerous peaks
> Her infinite variety

> Risky precipice.
> If the Fool falls
> Perhaps the rose will survive.

Tarot as Spiritual Pilgrimage

The Major Arcana are sometimes said to tell a story about Everyman, their journey through life, and the spiritual lessons encountered along the way. Have your students read some examples of this story, such as these two:

"The Fool's Journey" from *The Complete Book of Tarot* (Juliet Sharman-Burke, St. Martin's Press, 1996) starts in this way. "In our story, the hero is The Fool and we follow his life through childhood and education (The Magician), meeting his mortal parents (The Empress and The Emperor), his divine parents (The High Priestess and the Hierophant), his loves and conflicts (The Lovers and The Chariot), and his worldly trials of adulthood (Justice, Temperance, Strength, and The Hermit). . . ."

In *The Psychic Tarot* by Craig Junjulas (Morgan & Morgan, 1985), the story looks more like this: a young man leaves home to begin a journey in search of spiritual truth. Some call him a Fool, but he follows his inner guidance. He comes to a small school of the occult and trains as a Magician, acquiring skill, confidence, and initiative. Before he leaves, he seeks out the High Priestess, who shares her wisdom and knowledge. He treks to the city and is given an audience at the royal court . . . and so on.

Then ask your students to write their own version of the story, using every trump in order. This exercise can be done individually or in pairs or threes. For a variation, let the students change the order of the cards in any way that seems appropriate to them. You can also let students each try it on their own, then get together in threes and combine the best elements of each story. Be sure to allow plenty of time for everyone to read their stories and discuss them.

Once all the stories have been shared, you may wish to talk about common themes that occurred over and over (such as risk, obstacles, self-mastery, connections with a higher spirit, etc.) and put them up on a board or newsprint pad. Try to find all the elements common to every spiritual journey.

Simplest of all is to lay out the trumps in order, and then go round robin telling the story of the Fool's journey; each class member adds a few sentences based on the next card in sequence, then the next person continues the story.

Pathworking

Pathworking involves structured or guided meditation to integrate certain spiritual qualities and understandings into your life, based on the Qabalah's Tree of Life and (in this case) the Tarot.

The Tree of Life is a diagram or map of spiritual forces in the universe (see p. 235). Each spiritual force or focus is shown by a sephira, or sphere, as shown on the accompanying illustration. The lines between them are the paths, and each can correspond to a Tarot Major Arcanum.

Each pathworking meditation is a story that includes symbols special to that path and to its Tarot card. By going into a light trance and following the story, one hopes to emerge with a deeper understanding of that facet of reality and human spirituality, and the related card. The insight gained is not always on a conscious level, by the way; many of the elements of the meditation speak directly to the deep mind or subconscious.

There are several books on pathworking, and we especially recommend *Inner Landscapes* by Dolores Ashcroft-Nowicki (Aquarian Press, 1990). After you've experienced a set of pathworkings written by other people, and are familiar with the basic structure, you can begin to write your own pathworkings, incorporating the symbols that are most meaningful to you.

One way to use this tool with your class is to do one of the meditations at each class, and discuss it, and then advise your students to continue on their own between meetings. They can either read the pathworkings, or record them and play them back as they mkleditate.

Pathworking can be very powerful, so I recommend that you do no more than one meditation per week, to allow the full experience to become integrated before moving on to the next.

Teaching Various Gestalt Spreads

Ask each student to think of three questions they might explore through a Gestalt Tarot reading and write them down. Then lay out at least five different spreads on the floor and briefly describe each. Take each question in turn and discuss which spread might be most appropriate in addressing that question. Discuss the strengths and weaknesses of each spread and under what circumstances you might use it.

Creating Your Own Deck

This requires some serious advance preparation. Find a couple of hundred old magazines you don't mind cutting up, and that have lots of good pictures in them. *National Geographic* and other travel or science magazines are great, but throw in some news or general interest magazines as well, such as *Life*. Garage sales, yard sales, flea markets, and library sales are good sources.

Gather several pairs of scissors, some glue sticks, and a whole bunch of white card stock cut to Tarot-card size about 2.75" x 4.75". At this size you can get six from a standard letter-size sheet of card stock. You can find these at a local copy or print shop, where they have power cutters so all the cards are the same size and have straight edges.

Tell your students that they are going to create their own Tarot decks using pictures they find in magazines. They do not have to make a full seventy-eight-card deck; just as many cards as they can put together in whatever time you allot. If you want the activity more structured, ask them to make only the twenty-two

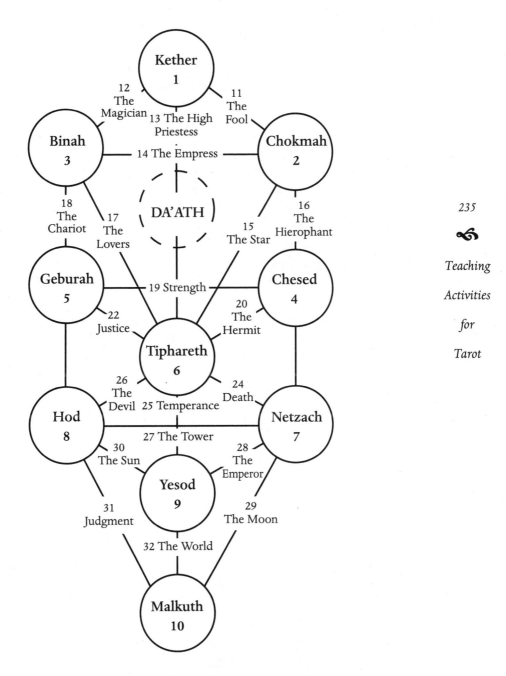

Tarot Pathworking

Major Arcana, using the best pictures they can find which convey the core themes of each card. Then hand out the materials and tell them to start cutting and pasting. Of course, half the fun is sharing your decks at the end of the class.

Living the Tarot

Sort out the trumps and court cards from a fairly standard Tarot deck. Ask each person to select a card and become that persona, either for a little while or for the duration of the class, assuming the costume and symbols of their figure.

This means having a good collection of costume pieces and props on hand. You will need a wand or staff, a sword, a chalice, and a pentacle. Other necessities include crowns, capes or cloaks, jewelry, a helmet, and miscellaneous robes, shawls, and extra fabric. A draped chair can become a throne. You may need to ask all the class members to bring boxes of dress-up materials and borrow special items such as swords, white mares, and oceans.

During the class, each person is to adopt the mannerisms and persona they imagine their figure to have, and each must be addressed by their title. Each in turn can introduce themselves and explain their philosophy and strengths to the group.

Alternatively, have just three or four people assume card personas, and form a panel. The other class members can ask the panel's opinions on world issues or personal questions. They can "be" different cards, or all the same card.

Designing New Cards

Ask each student to design a new trump card to represent a quality from the list below. They can draw and color the card; make a small collage of pictures cut from magazines; or come up with the idea and symbolism, then ask someone with artistic talent to do the final rendition. Choose from these themes or any others that may be relevant to the students:

Abundance	Courage	Empathy
Affection	Courtesy	Enlightenment
Aggression	Creativity	Faith
Anger	Cunning	Fear
Caution	Curiosity	Foolishness
Communication	Despair	Friendship
Compassion	Destruction	Generosity
Conflict	Discretion	Good Cheer
Confusion	Doubt	Greed

Growth	Loyalty	Sloth
Harmony	Lust	Spontaneity
Haste	Obedience	Stability
Healing	Obstacles	Success
Health	Order	Suspicion
Hedonism	Peace	The Social Contract
Helpfulness	Psychic Ability	Thrift
High Energy	Reverence	Trickiness
Hope	Romance	Trust
Imagination	Self-Defeat	Victory
Innocence	Self-Respect	Wanderlust
Inventiveness	Sensuality	Weirdness
Joy	Serendipity	Will
Kindness	Serenity	Wisdom
Knowledge	Silence	

Afterward, share your cards and discuss how you chose the figures, colors, and symbols for each.

Countervision

Everyone sits in a circle. One student pulls a card from the deck and offers their personal interpretation; the next two people to the left must each offer a contrary or alternative meaning (see chapters 4 and 5). Then the person immediately to the left of the first selects a card, and the process continues around the circle. This is especially useful in preparation for practicing Gestalt Tarot.

Challenges in Reading

Take turns giving Gestalt readings to each other, with the querent role-playing difficult situations you might encounter reading for others, such as those listed in chapter 13:

The Skeptic	The Doomsayer
The Monosyllabic Response	The New Age Child Of Light
The Talking-Head Analyst	The Tarot Expert
The Guru Seeker	The Scaredy Cat
The Passive Client	The Naysayer
The Deadbeat .	The Omen Watcher

After a few minutes of role-playing, stop the action and ask others to comment on how the situation was handled and what they might have done instead.

Tarot Message Gifts to One Another

All stand in a circle with their own decks and sort out the trumps. Then each student draws a trump from his or her deck and verbally offers its gift to the others in the group. An example: Sabrina draws The Chariot from her deck, shows it to the rest of the circle, and says: "To me this stands for the power that is ours when we act in balance. When you can harness the energies of both mercy and severity, masculine and feminine, light and dark, and guide them with your wisdom and intuition as the charioteer guides his horses—then you can accomplish anything. I offer each of you balance and power."

Outline for a Basic Tarot Class

This class is designed for people who are beginners or at least fairly inexperienced in Tarot. It might be accomplished in two or three hours, if you present it as a lecture and cut out the activities; or it could easily be extended to fill a day or a series of evening classes.

Welcome and Introductions

> The instructor and their background
> The students, their backgrounds and experience with Tarot
> Activity: Go round robin and have each student introduce themselves

The Origins and History of Tarot

> Various theories: Atlantis, Egypt, the Gnostics, etc.
> Early decks and writings on Tarot
> Activity: Lecture only

The Uses of Tarot

> Predictive / fortunetelling
> Self-exploration and spiritual growth
> Decision-making
> Counseling
> Magick
> Recreation
> Activity: Demonstrate a simple Tarot magick spell

The Structure of the Deck

The Major Arcana and the spiritual pilgrimage
The Minor Arcana
    Court cards
    Pip cards
The standard and variations
Activity: Have students lay out the Major Arcana in order, and then the
    four suits in order, on the floor or a large table

Decks Available Today

Visconti-Sforza and other reproductions of early decks
The *Rider-Waite* deck and its offshoots: *Morgan-Greer, Robin Wood,* etc.
Golden Dawn decks: The *Crowley-Thoth Tarot, New Golden Dawn,* etc.
Feminist decks: *Motherpeace, Daughters of the Moon*; Art decks: *Dali, Pomo,* etc.
Ethnic decks: Egyptian, Norse, Native American, Mayan, etc.
Animal decks: *Celtic Dragon, Cat People, Crow's Magick, Shapeshifter,* etc.
Cards inspired by the Tarot: *Celtic Tree Oracle, Goddess* cards, *Shamanic*
    Animals, etc.
Activity: Show examples, and let students share favorite decks that they have
    brought with them

Some Basic Spreads

The Celtic Cross Spread
The Three-Card Spread
The Gestalt Spread and Condensed Version
Other personal favorites
Activity: Let each student memorize a different spread, then practice in pairs

Interpreting the Cards

The book method (memorized meanings)
The psychic or intuitive method
The Gestalt method
Activity: Demonstrate each method briefly, using three different students as
    querents, but the same card with all of them

Sources for Decks

Local metaphysical bookstores
Catalogs (Llewellyn Publications, U.S. Games Systems, AGMüller, etc.)

Internet shopping
Activity: Show catalogs

Recommended Reading and Research Sources

Bring along a handout with a good bibliography and a list of good Tarot
  websites
Discussion of favorite books on Tarot
Internet websites related to Tarot
Periodicals and associations
Activity: Show books and discuss favorites

Closing Circle

Activity: Each person offers a gift to the group, based on a Tarot card

Hand out feedback forms after each class (What did you like best/worst? How
could I improve? etc.), and take the advice given, so your presentation will improve each time.

Basic Outline for Series of Tarot Classes

These class outlines use primarily the exercises described in this chapter and other
information in this book. The six-class program is designed for a small group of
people who have prior experience with Tarot. Depending on the number of students, their Tarot backgrounds, and how deeply they get into the activities, you
may need to extend the series to as many as twelve classes in order to get through
all the material.

Class One

Welcome and Introductions
Tarot Get-Acquainted Exercise
Origins and History of Tarot
The Uses of Tarot
The Structure of the Deck
Exploring Different Decks
Card Games with Tarot
Sources for Tarot Cards
Homework Assignment: Purchase or Borrow a Tarot Deck and Get to
  Know It
Closing: Tarot Message Gifts

Class Two

Welcome
Comparing Deck Imagery
Interpreting the Cards
Gestalt Tarot
The Fool's Journey: Tarot as Spiritual Pilgrimage
Exploring One Card in Depth
Homework: Designing Your Own Card
Closing: Tarot Message Gifts

Class Three

Welcome
Sharing the Cards Designed at Home
Some Basic Spreads
Practice with Partners
Countervision Exercise
Homework: Creating a Personal Trump
Closing: Tarot Message Gifts

Class Four

Welcome
Sharing Personal Trumps
Living the Tarot
Creating Your Own Deck
Homework: Make More Cards at Home
Closing: Tarot Message Gifts

Class Five

Welcome
Sharing More Cards Made at Home
Challenging Clients Role-Plays
Pathworking
Homework: Continue Pathworking on Your Own (no more than one
    pathworking per week, please)
Closing: Tarot Message Gifts

Class Six

Welcome

Tarot Magick: Practice a Spell

Haiku Poems

Recommended Books and Other Resources

Closing: Tarot Message Gifts

When the classes are completed, you may want to give some form of recognition to students who have attended the whole series. You can design a certificate on your home computer, or ask a friend who is good at graphic design to do it. Obtain some nice paper from an office supply store, photocopy shop, or printing establishment, and you can print personalized certificates on your computer printer.

If some of the students are interested, they can continue meeting as a self-guided study group to practice readings and share feedback.

Chapter 14

Taroc Magick

Tarot is primarily a tool for divination; that is, for revealing hidden knowledge and predicting probable futures by extrapolating present trends. However, the rich symbolism of the Tarot can also be used in magick and ritual.

This is not the place for a detailed description of magick; the essentials of magick are covered in Amber's book, *True Magick: A Beginner's Guide* (Llewellyn, 1990). Suffice it to say that we are talking about real magick, magick-with-a-*k* to distinguish it from tricks, stage illusions, or fantasy-novel magic. The distinguished magician William E. Butler has defined it as "the art of effecting changes in consciousness at will." It might also be called the art of changing reality through the disciplined use of imagination, emotion, will, and directed psychic energy.

The Echics of Magick

Wise and experienced magicians already know what I am about to explain in this section, but it must be said for the benefit of those who are new to the Art. Magick of any kind must be used ethically and responsibly, or it will hurt you.

There is a natural law called the *Law of Return*. Simply stated, it says that whatever energy you send out will return to you—multiplied. Sometimes it is called the *Threefold Law*, meaning that the returning energy will be three times as strong as that which you sent out. If you send out healing energy, you will receive healing when you need it. If you send energy for protection, you will be protected. If you send energy to harm or control another, you will be harmed or controlled.

This idea is very ancient. It is implied in the Golden Rule: "Do unto others as you would have others do unto you." More recently we hear it as "What goes around, comes around."

We cannot predict the timetable; the energy might rebound in thirty seconds or in ten years. However, there are no exceptions; you cannot shield yourself from the returning power, or turn it aside, or escape it in any way. What you send out, comes back to you—period.

To the Law of Return, I would add this counsel from the Craft of the Wise: "An ye harm none, do as ye will." That is, follow your heart as long as no one is harmed (including yourself!). An extension of this principle says that you should never do magick to affect another person without their express permission. We cannot decide for another what might help or harm them; only they can make that decision. This means that we do not even do healing magick for someone unless they have requested it.

Therefore, when you do Tarot magick, do it ONLY for yourself or your friends who have asked for help, and NEVER work magick to harm, manipulate, or control anyone else.

That said, on to the spells. Remember, you are using Gestalt Tarot techniques, so use the images in the deck as they appear; do not use the traditional meanings.

Self-Transformation

Most of us want to grow; to become stronger, wiser, more loving people. To accomplish this we may do exercise programs, educate ourselves, read self-help books, and follow spiritual practices such as prayer, yoga, meditation, saying the rosary, or practicing the Middle Pillar.

One way of enhancing all these is to create a Major Arcanum Tarot card for yourself; one that depicts you as the central figure . . . but you as you could be, not as you are.

If you have some talent for illustration, you can illustrate the card yourself. Otherwise, find a friend or acquaintance with the necessary skill and ask for help. You could even commission a graphic designer or fine artist to do the job with your guidance.

Begin by making a list of all the qualities you want to have, or enhance in yourself. They might include some of those listed following this paragraph (see p. 245). Then sort through your favorite Tarot deck and pull out all the cards that remind you of the qualities you want. Make a list of the cards and what, specifically, you like about each one. The colors? The way the central figure is standing?

The clothing? The expression on the face? The landscape in the background? Other symbols in the card such as animals, birds, plants, or tools?

Affection	Fairness	Musical Talent
Alertness	Friendliness	Perceptivity
Athleticism	Generosity	Prosperity
Charisma	Gracefulness	Prudence
Cheerfulness	Health	Quickness
Cleanliness	Honor	Reliability
Communication	Humor	Sensuality
Compassion	Industry	Sobriety
Courage	Intellect	Strength
Courtesy	Joy	Thoughtfulness
Creativity	Kindness	Thrift
Daring	Leadership	Truthfulness
Endurance	Lovingness	Understanding
Energy	Loyalty	Wisdom

Add to the list anything else you can think of that symbolizes the qualities you want. An eagle for clear vision? A crescent moon for intuition? A crown for a commanding personality? A heart for compassion? A dog for loyalty?

Once you have your list completed, you can either begin to sketch your own card, or show it to your artist friend and explain what you want. My notes looked something like this:

A Major Arcanum Card for Amber K

Qualities I want to enhance: health and fitness, far-sightedness/vision, high energy, and playfulness and joy in life.

Symbols I found in my favorite deck: slender, standing figures; an eagle; mountains; a fish in a chalice; swords; the sun and the moon; a white horse.

Card design: A tall, slender, blonde woman stands holding the halter of a beautiful white horse. A sword is strapped behind the saddle. The woman is wearing black trousers and a black tunic with a crescent-moon on the left breast. They stand in a mountain meadow covered with wildflowers, the sun is high, and an eagle soars overhead. She gazes off into far mountain vistas, smiling.

Note: I don't see a good way to include the fish in the chalice. I'm hardly going to ride a horse carrying that. Maybe the flowers will do for "playfulness and joy," or maybe I can think of a way to include dolphin symbolism. A colorful banner with a dolphin on it? Maybe the mountains are on the coast and the meadow is overlooking the ocean, where a dolphin plays?

You may need to go through several sketches to arrive at the final version. The card should be large, perhaps as big as 8½" x 11" (a standard sheet of paper). The final version should be rendered in full color on illustration board or even canvas, if you're painting in oils or acrylics. However, you may prefer water colors, pastels, ink, or colored pencils.

When the card is complete, charge it in a magick circle using drumming, dancing, chanting, or whatever method you like to raise energy. Then assume the same position as the figure in the card, close your eyes, and vividly imagine every detail in the card. Inhale the energy of the card.

Every day following, spend a few minutes meditating quietly on the card. In the morning, ask yourself, "What must I do today to become a little closer to the image in the card? To become myself as I might be, myself as I will be." In the evening, ask yourself, "What could I have done better today . . . and what can I do better tomorrow?" Don't berate yourself, simply acknowledge where you could have improved, and then vow to do better tomorrow.

Self-Cleansing

All of us, from time to time, live through an experience that leaves us feeling less than clean. Perhaps you were in a relationship in which you were used, or were not honest. Perhaps you did something else that wasn't quite ethical. Perhaps you have been living an unhealthy lifestyle involving drugs, too much alcohol, or junk food. Whatever the cause, you can cleanse yourself and start fresh.

Choose the card that best represents you, or you as you plan to become. For one full day, preferably the day of the full moon, carry the card with you at all times. Frequently take it out and spend a minute meditating on it; think about why the card is like you, and why you are like the card.

The night of the full moon, sleep with the card under your pillow or on a nightstand where you can see it easily. The object is to create a bond between you and the card, so that it becomes an "object link," and what is done to the card is done to you.

The next day, as the moon begins to wane, begin a cleansing fast (first check with your physician if you have never fasted or have any health conditions that might be negatively affected). Drink nothing but liquids for a full day and night, or up to three days if you are used to fasting. This could include pure water, natural fruit juices, and nourishing soups or broths.

At the end of the fast, set up your personal altar. On it, have a bowl of pure water, a container of salt, a candle, some incense, and a symbol of Spirit (perhaps a religious statuette or picture), as well as the Tarot card. Then take a bath in either warm or slightly cool water, depending on the weather and your mood. You may want to do this by candlelight, with relaxing music playing.

Afterward put on a clean, loose robe (white is best) and sit quietly before your altar for a short time, breathing deeply. Imagine that with every in-breath, you are inhaling the purest air in the world. With every out-breath, you are expelling anything your body, mind, heart, and spirit don't want: impurities, toxins, bad feelings, negative thoughts, and so on.

- Take your Tarot card and sprinkle salt on it, saying "I cleanse you and myself by the power of Earth"

- Pass it through the incense smoke, saying "I cleanse you and myself by the power of Air"

- Pass it above the candle flame, saying "I cleanse you and myself by the power of Fire"

- Pass it over the bowl of water, saying "I cleanse you and myself by the power of Water"

- Hold it before your Spirit symbol, saying "I cleanse you and myself by the power of Spirit"

Look at the card and say, "Thus are you cleansed and purified, absolved and forgiven, beginning again as a new thing. Thus am I cleansed and purified, absolved and forgiven, beginning again as a new person. So mote it be, so it is, so it shall be from this day forward."

Later, when you feel the magick has been successful, say to the card: "With thanks, I release you from this magickal connection." Put it back in the deck.

The Element You Need

We are all blends of various qualities and traits. If you would like to achieve a better balance in your personality, you can use an Elemental system to achieve it. Look at the following list of Elements and their attributes, and give yourself a score from 1 through 10 on each set of qualities. Average the numbers in each list to find out how strongly you personify each Element.

The Element of Earth

Scores:

9	Solid, reliable, honest, consistent
9	Physically fit, healthy, strong, aware of your body
7	Tough, enduring, resilient, filled with stamina
3	Prosperous, good job, wealthy in material possessions

Your Average Score for Earth: 28 / 7

The Element of Air

Scores:

9	Thoughtful, intelligent, curious
9	Imaginative, mentally creative, a problem-solver
8	Mentally self-disciplined, able to focus and concentrate
8	Highly educated, broadly knowledgeable, well informed

Your Average Score for Air: 34 - 8.

The Element of Fire

Scores:

9	Passionate, intense, willful, strong desires
9	High energy, a doer, mover and shaker
8	Goal oriented, self-directed, ambitious
5	Wanting to cleanse, purify, and simplify

Your Average Score for Fire: 31 - 7.9

The Element of Water

Scores:

9	Sensitive, emotional, in touch with your feelings
9	Intuitive, holistic, grasping situations with only partial facts
9	Flowing, persistent, relentless, moving around obstacles
9	Compassionate, caring, loving, nurturing

Your Average Score for Water: 36 -9

The Element of Spirit

Scores:

8	A sense of balance, rightness, and serenity
9	A mind that travels through space and time. Dreamer, visionary, mystic
5	A powerful sense of connectedness with all living things, and with the Source of all
5	An awareness of your own sacredness

Your Average Score for Spirit: 27 - 6.9

Average Scores

EARTH ___7___ AIR ___8.5___ FIRE ___7.9___ WATER ___9___ SPIRIT ___6.9___

What is your lowest average score? Are one or more Elements definitely out of balance with the others? Achieving balance is possible, if you want it. It is a life-long task, but here is a little Tarot magick to help you along the way. Do it during a waxing moon for best effect.

Choose a card to represent yourself as you are now. Place under it the card that looks to you like a perfectly balanced person (some people choose "Temperance" or "The Star"). In a wide circle around these, place all the cards from the suit you are *weakest* in (Earth = Pentacles, Discs or Coins; Air = Swords; Fire = Wands or Rods; Water = Cups; Spirit = the Major Arcana, using only the ones that feel positive to you).

Now charge the cards by drumming (Earth), singing (Air), chanting (Water), or dancing (Fire), using the element you are strongest in, and begin to slowly bring the cards of the outer circle in toward the center. If you wish you can chant:

> "Air I am, Fire I am, Water, Earth, and Spirit I am."

As you do this, visualize yourself in daily life, but strongly exhibiting the qualities of the Element you need. Breathe deeply.

When all the cards have reached the center, gather them up with the two original cards in the middle of the stack. Raise power one more time, using the means of your "weakest" element, but building on the power you raised before. Around the cards, tie a ribbon of the appropriate Elemental color (Earth = brown or forest green, Air = light blue, Fire = orange or red, Water = light green or deep blue, Spirit = violet or purple). Keep them on your altar until the full moon, then raise power to charge them once more, before thanking the Elements, blessing the cards, and returning them to the deck.

Circle of Change Spell for Self-Transformation

This spell can be done at any phase of the moon. During the waning moon you would concentrate on banishing negative things from your life, and during a waxing moon you would focus on bringing positive new things into your life.

Choose a card to represent yourself as you are now, and another that symbolizes the way you wish to be. Place them on your altar or working surface with the "Present You" card on top, and the "Desired You" card beneath it. Now pick seven to nine other cards that represent the undesired energies now in your life, and an equal number symbolizing the qualities or energies you want.

Place the negative cards in a tight circle around the self cards. Put the positive cards in a larger circle around them.

Each night just before you go to bed, *or* each morning soon after you rise, meditate on the spread for a short time. Choose a negative card representing something you want to release from your life and think about how you have supported that negative energy, even if only by passively allowing it in your life. Then remove the card from the spread and put it away in the deck. Or, if you prefer, throw it across the room or into the trash, or tear it to shreds. It's not a cheap way to do magick, but the drama is very satisfying to your younger self.

Now choose a positive card showing what you do want in your life. Think about what behavior would support that change, and choose a very specific action you will perform to invite that energy into your life. (For example, if you have a card representing prosperity through a new job, then tell your friends you're looking, or call the place you would like to work and ask about openings, or update your resumé.) Charge that card with drumming, breathing, chanting, or whatever means you prefer, and move it into the place vacated by the negative card.

Repeat this process each day, until all the negative cards have been replaced by positive. On the last day, remove the "Present You" card from the center, revealing the "Desired You" beneath it. Charge the entire spread with energy, then go out and act in accord.

A Journey of Personal Growth

This spell deals with the most basic question: "Who am I?" And it leads inexorably to the next: "Am I who I want to be?" . . . and if not . . . "Who would I rather be?" . . . "Am I willing to do the work to become the person I want to be?". . . and . . . "What must I do to become that person, the potential Me?"

Choose the Tarot card which best symbolizes you as you are now. Perhaps you could start by asking yourself which suit is your strength: Swords (intellect and imagination), Wands (energy and purpose), Cups (emotion and intuition), or Pentacles (body, the Earth, material things). Or perhaps there is a Major Arcanum which represents you. Go through the deck quickly and pick out several cards which seem likely possibilities, then go back and choose the best one to symbolize yourself. If in doubt, ask a close friend or family member which card is most like you.

Now choose a card to represent your potential self. You can be modest in your desires, or quite grandiose; you can be almost anyone you want to be, providing you are willing to work at it!

Now you need to make a "journey" sequence of cards from where you are to where you want to be. Write down the steps required; if you can brainstorm with a good friend, so much the better. Then put them in order. Which step, taken first, would make the others easier to achieve? Hint: solve your biggest problem first. Very often you must deal with a pressing health issue, or a relationship crisis, or get a job and some income, before you can usefully work on anything else.

Choose a card to represent each step in the process, and line them up on your altar in the correct order between the "Present You" and the "Future You" cards. Then meditate in front of the altar every morning, using the time to plan action that will move you toward the next card in line. The action can be small: as easy as skipping your usual doughnut this morning, making a phone call to get a bit of information, or updating your resumé to help you apply for a better job. But do one little thing every day.

Note: to reinforce the effect of this spell, keep a diary on your altar next to the journey cards. Each evening, write down the thing you did to move ahead on the journey and how you felt after doing it. If you miss a day, don't rebuke yourself—just be sure to do it the following day.

Enjoy the process, and say hello to your new self.

Achieving Your Goal

It is sometimes easy to set goals, but not so easy to achieve them. This spell is a simple way to help remind and motivate you. First, choose a Self card to represent yourself. If you are feeling less than good about yourself at the moment, don't choose a card representing your weaker side. The card must remind you of yourself at your best.

Then choose another card to represent your goal—as long as the goal is not a relationship with another specific person, since manipulative magick is unethical and will backfire.

Now pick a third card to become your *horse*; that is, the energy that will carry you forward to your goal. The Chariot or the Six of Wands are two obvious possibilities, if you are literal-minded. However, the horse could also be Strength, to represent courage; or the Six of Swords, to symbolize the strength to move on in spite of sorrow; or the Three of Cups, for a network of friends; or the Ten of Wands, for the ability to handle multiple tasks; or the Seven of Pentacles, for hard work, and so on.

At the new moon, place your goal card in the center of the altar. Place your Self card, the "rider," on the "horse" card at one edge of the altar. Every day, soon after you arise, sit before the altar and meditate on what you will do that day to move toward achieving your goal. Then move the horse and rider cards an inch closer to the goal card.

If something obstructs your progress, choose a card to represent the obstacle and put it on the altar. Meditate on how you can overcome it or move around it. Add other cards to represent resources you have, or friends you can call upon. The important thing is to keep the horse and rider moving, even if you have to take a long and winding route. Continue until you reach the goal.

Magick for Vibrant Health

When the moon is new, place a card chosen to represent yourself in the center of the spread. Under it, place the Ace of Pentacles. In a circle around it, place cards chosen to represent the factors involved in health and wellness: clean air, pure water, natural sunlight, good nutrition, exercise, peaceful sleep, relaxation, love, self-esteem, and anything else you can think of. The card representing the factor you are *most* in need of should be placed on the ascendant, or directly above the Self card.

Now charge the spread with chanting, dancing, drumming, or in whatever way you like to raise energy. Gather the spread together, with the Self card approximately in the center of the stack, and place it on your altar. Each day, preferably in the morning or at noon, lay the cards out and charge them again, until the full moon.

And of course . . . act in accord! Take action daily to improve your diet, reduce stress, or whatever else you need to support the magick and improve your health.

The Circle of Protection

Choose a card to represent yourself. Then take each of the Knights and place them in the appropriate quarters around your Self card: the Knight of Swords to the East, the Knight of Wands to the South, the Knight of Cups to the West, and the Knight of Pentacles to the North.

As you place each Knight, charge and consecrate it with the appropriate element. Begin by brushing the Knight of Swords with a feather, or move it through the smoke of incense, or slide it along the blade of an actual sword; or do all three. Hold it up to the East, and in a ringing voice proclaim: "Knight of the East, Power of Air! Protect me and mine from all perils that come from the East, and all threats to my mind! As I will, so mote it be!"

Take the Knight of Wands and move it just above a candle flame, or slide it along a wand or magickal staff; or do both. Hold it up to the South, and in a ringing voice proclaim: "Knight of the South, Power of Fire! Protect me and mine from all perils that come from the South, and all threats to my energy and purpose! As I will, so mote it be!"

Touch the Knight of Cups with a finger dipped in water or wine, or move it above a filled chalice; or do both. Hold it up to the West, and in a ringing voice proclaim: "Knight of the West, Power of Water! Protect me and mine from all perils that come from the West, and all threats to my heart and emotions! As I will, so mote it be!"

Place the Knight of Pentacles on a consecrated pentacle, or sprinkle it with salt, or place it under a stone; or do all three. Hold it up to the North, and in a ringing voice proclaim: "Knight of the North, Power of Earth! Protect me and mine from all perils that come from the North, and all threats to my body, home, and possessions! As I will, so mote it be!"

Choose a card to represent the Power of Spirit, such as the High Priestess or Justice. Anoint it with a special oil, or ring a chime next to it, or do both. Hold it up in the center, and in a ringing voice proclaim: "Dweller at the Center of All, Power of Spirit! Protect me and mine from all perils that come from the compass 'round, and all threats to my spirit and soul! As I will, so mote it be!" Place this card over your Self card.

Leave the pattern in place until you feel the danger has passed, then thank the Powers and cards, ask the Powers for continued protection, and return the cards to the deck.

Collapsing the House of Ill Fortune

If it seems everything has recently been going wrong in your life, choose three sets of cards for this spell. First pick several cards to represent all your misfortunes. You will need at least five cards, but more would be better. These might be cards such as:

The Tower	The Devil	The Moon
The Wheel of Fortune	The Five of Cups	The Eight of Cups
The Five of Pentacles	The Five of Wands	The Seven of Wands
The Ten of Wands	The Four of Swords	The Five of Swords
The Six of Swords	The Eight of Swords	The Nine of Swords
The Ten of Swords		

Use these to build your "house of ill fortune," gently leaning and stacking them into a three-dimensional box or tower.

Then pick the cards representing the way you would like your life to be and a Self card to represent you. Take all the remaining royal cards (Empress, Emperor, Kings, Queens, and Knights) and place them in a stack.

Meditate and visualize your life the way it has been. Then visualize change, and the way your life could be. Now call upon the forces you believe in: gods and goddesses, spirit helpers and guides, animal totems, or guardian angels. In your own words, ask them to help change your life for the better.

Inhale their combined power, and with a huge breath, blow down the house of ill fortune. Pick up the stack of royal cards and sweep away the remnants of the house. Pick up the cards symbolizing your new life, and create a new pattern on the spot where the house was—perhaps a circle with your Self card in the center. Thank the powers that have helped you, and make your plans to act in accord and manifest your new life.

Prosperity and Abundance

Choose a card to represent yourself and another to represent poverty or scarcity; such as the Five of Cups. Choose all the cards you can find to represent the kind of abundance you want, and stack them up. The following suggestions are based on the images in the *Morgan-Greer* deck. The deck you use may suggest other options. Remember, use the images as they appear, not the traditional meanings. Some possibilities are:

- Bountiful friendship and love: the Two, Three, Ten, and Ace of Cups, and the Lovers

- Money and material wealth: the Six, Nine, King, Queen, and Ace of Pentacles

- Children: the Six of Cups

- Home: the Four of Wands

- Career or livelihood: the Eight of Pentacles

- Abundant wisdom and psychic sensitivity: the Four of Pentacles

- Bountiful harvest of any kind: the Seven of Pentacles

- Abundance in general: the Empress, Emperor, Sun, and World

Place the poverty card next to the Self card, and think for a moment what has been lacking in your life. Is it money, or love, or food, or shelter, or a career, or opportunity? Think of three actions you can take to change the situation. Speak them aloud, making yourself a promise, beginning with the words, "I will. . . ." Then pick up the poverty card and throw it across the room as hard as you can!

Take the abundance cards and surround your Self card with them. Charge them with drumming, dancing, a favorite song, or this chant:

> *I am the Sword cutting free from scarcity,*
> *I am the living Wand, with green leaves sprouting,*
> *I am the Cup with wine overflowing,*
> *I am the Pentacle heaped with the Earth's bounty,*
> *I am Spirit, abundant and eternal!*

Follow through on your promise of action. Return the poverty card to the deck, at the bottom. Leave the pattern in place and recharge it often until prosperity comes, then thank the cards and return them to the deck.

Charging a Tarot Talisman

Pick a card to serve as your role model. Find or make a talisman to represent that card. For example, the Queen of Wands has sunflowers in the design; pick some sunflower petals, dry them, and place them in a tiny vial or pouch along with a scrap of yellow cloth and a bit of oak leaf or oak wood. Here are some other cards you might choose, and potential materials for an amulet or talisman:

- Strength: A tiny picture of a lion or the Leo astrological symbol and a scrap of white cloth

- The Magician: A white lily petal and a red rose petal

- Queen of Cups: A pearl and a small shell

- Temperance: A white feather and a tiny red fire triangle

- The Chariot: A black thread and a white, intertwined and wrapped in a scrap of royal blue cloth

- Queen of Swords: A red rose petal, a pearl, and a thorn

- King of Swords: An acorn, a holly berry, and a grain of wheat

- Queen of Pentacles: An oak leaf or acorn, and a polished carnelian cabochon

You can also buy a miniature Tarot deck (available from U.S. Games Systems, through your nearest metaphysical store) and use the actual card as part of your talisman.

Once you have created the amulet or talisman, wear it or carry it in a pocket as you cast a circle and assume the same position as the figure in the card. Using costumes and props helps; if you can dress like the figure, or carry a staff or sword or cup or whatever, so much the better.

Next chant to raise power and charge the talisman you're wearing. You can make up your own appropriate chant; it does not have to be long, nor great poetry. Here's an example:

> *I call in chant the Queen of Swords, hearken now to all my words;*
> *Steady gaze and lifted head, stalwart blade and roses red,*
> *She is me and I am she, as I will, so mote it be!*

At the peak of power, charge the talisman, then ground the excess energy, thank the Powers, and open the circle. Carry your amulet or talisman with you always.

Adding Herbs, Woods, and Stones

If you have chosen a card to represent your goal, not only can you charge it when you select it, but you can also boost the charge with herbs and stones. To choose an herb, refer to a book on herb magick such as the *Encyclopedia of Magical Herbs* by Scott Cunningham (Llewellyn, 1985). Here are just a few recommendations:

- Courage: Mullein, Thyme, Yarrow

- Employment: Devil's Shoestring, Lucky Hand, Pecan

- Fertility: Fig, Rice, Sunflower

- Friendships: Lemon, Passion Flower, Sweetpea

- Healing: Allspice, Bay, Garlic

- Health: Marjoram, Nutmeg, Sassafras

- Love: Lemon Balm, Basil, Chamomile

- Mental powers: Eyebright, Rosemary, Spearmint

- Peace and harmony: Lavender, Vervain, Violet

- Psychic powers: Celery, Peppermint, Saffron

- Spirituality: African Violet, Cinnamon, Gardenia

- Strength: Mugwort, Plantain, Thistle

- Success: Clover, Ginger, High John the Conqueror

- Wealth: Cinnamon, Dill, Mint

- Wisdom: Iris, Sage, Sunflower

You may also use the magickal powers of various woods to strengthen a Tarot spell. Some correspondences, in part from *Tree Medicine, Tree Magic* by Ellen Evert Hopman (Phoenix, 1991), include the following:

- Courage: Oak, Ash, Birch, Rowan, Hawthorn, Holly

- Employment: Birch, Larch, Oak, Hawthorn, Poplar, Cedar

- Fertility: Oak, Pine, Apple, Hawthorn, Walnut

- Friendships: Cedar, Apple, Willow

- Healing: Oak, Walnut, Pine, Ash, Willow, Holly, Birch, Rowan, Eucalyptus, Cedar, Elder, Apple

- Health: Acorn, Holly, Eucalyptus, Poplar

- Love: Ash, Willow, Maple, Apple, Chestnut, Cedar, Walnut

- Mental powers: Holly, Hawthorn, Walnut

- Peace and harmony: Larch

- Psychic powers: Cedar, Willow, Holly, Eucalyptus, Larch

- Spirituality: Poplar, Oak

- Strength: Oak, Apple, Poplar, Pine, Ash

- Success: Oak, Ash, Cedar, Walnut, Poplar

- Wealth: Cedar, Elder, Poplar, Pine, Maple

- Wisdom: Apple, Hawthorn

When in doubt add cedar, the wood most closely associated with Tarot.

Various stones and crystals hold a magickal charge and can release it into the Tarot card gradually over a long period of time. Here are some selections from the *Encyclopedia of Crystal, Gem & Metal Magic* by Scott Cunningham (Llewellyn, 1988) and *Stone Power* by Dorothee Mella (Warner Books, 1986), as well as from our own experience:

- Courage: Banded Agate, Tiger's Eye, Aquamarine, Carnelian, Sardonyx
- Employment: Plume Agate, Sapphire
- Fertility: Moss Agate, Amber, Geode, Pearl, Chalcedony, Mother-of-Pearl
- Friendships: Chrysoprase, Pink Tourmaline, Turquoise, Garnet
- Healing: Quartz Crystal, Carnelian, Bloodstone, Holy Stone
- Health: Agate, Amber, Coral, Jet, Turquoise, Amethyst
- Love: Amber, Beryl, Pearl, Rhodocrosite, Chrysocolla, Topaz
- Mental powers: Aventurine, Emerald, Zircon, Quartz Crystal, Fluorite, Azurite, Malachite, Citrine, Lapis Lazuli
- Peace and harmony: Rose Quartz, Sapphire, Turquoise, Aquamarine, Chalcedony, Sodalite
- Psychic powers: Moonstone, Lapis Lazuli, Aquamarine, Emerald, Azurite
- Spirituality: Amethyst, Lapis Lazuli, Moonstone, Calcite, Diamond, Sugilite
- Strength: Agate, Amber, Beryl, Bloodstone, Diamond, Garnet, Hematite, Tiger Iron, Banded Agate
- Success: Amazonite, Chrysoprase, Marble, Bloodstone, Malachite, Aventurine, Tourmaline, Sapphire
- Wealth: Sunstone, Calcite, Chrysoprase, Mother-of-Pearl, Peridot, Green Tourmaline
- Wisdom: Amethyst, Jade, Lapis Lazuli, Chyrsocolla, Coral, Jade, Sodalite, Sugilite

Cunningham's book also presents the idea of a "Stone Tarot," using various gemstones to symbolize the Major Arcana. He has a list of stones as suggested associations with each card, or you can come up with your own.

The Tarot is a powerful tool for magick, but remember to use it only for positive and ethical purposes, or that same power can backfire on you.

Chapter 15

Summary and Conclusion

This is Gestalt Tarot. It is a method for achieving self-understanding using Tarot cards as a tool, with the reader as facilitator. It helps the querent answer questions such as "Who am I?" "What do I want and need?" "Where am I going?" and "What must I do to take responsibility for my life, and turn it toward goals I value?"

By its very nature, Gestalt is expansive. The process resists narrow focus, superficial explanations, and easy answers. It encourages us to explore the querent as a whole, and their problems and questions in the context of their entire life.

Gestalt Tarot requires the reader to dedicate to a discovery process, and to abjure personal bias or prejudice as to the results. In this way it is like good science. A competent scientist does not go into a research project feeling certain what the results *should* be—they follow the scientific method and allow the data to speak for itself. In the same way, a competent Gestalt Tarot reader does not decide what the cards *should* mean for a particular querent—they allow querents to find their own meanings, and to decide how to use the information in their lives.

So the reader's focus is entirely on keeping the process pure, while they remain completely objective and neutral regarding the content that emerges. A reader must not care whether Sally marries Harry or dumps him, whether Ralph takes a job with Amalgamated Smelting or Pizza Shack, whether Doris moves to Tibet or stays in New Jersey. The reader cares only that Sally, Ralph, and Doris discover their own truths and come to clarity about what they want and where they are headed.

259

Gestalt Tarot leads querents to understand their lives and make their own decisions. Thus it is the antithesis of power-over systems, external authority, the ceding of control to experts, and the entire father-knows-best paradigm. Instead, it is all about responsibility, independence, and respect. The reader must say with a whole heart, "You are responsible for understanding and directing your own life. You are free to do as you think best. I respect your choices."

Some would call this the Aquarian Ethic. It rests on the belief that we—all humanity, perhaps all life forms—are a community of spiritual equals. That we are all inherently and equally valuable in the eyes of Deity and, more importantly, in the eyes of one another. That, therefore, no one has the right to direct or control the life of another, beyond what is necessary for self-protection. That our attitude toward other beings should be one of profound respect. That our duty toward one another should be, first of all, to take responsibility for our own lives as mature, self-directed adults; and second, to encourage others to do the same.

Not everyone wants to be empowered. Denial, helplessness, dependency, and victimhood can be seductive and even rewarding in some ways. Therefore, some people will reject tools that require personal assumption of responsibility, such as Gestalt Tarot. They would rather be told how to live and what to do next, and they may seek a Tarot reader who will oblige them. They are allowed that freedom, that choice.

But for the rest of us, who cherish our independence and accept the attached responsibilities with open eyes, and who passionately want a world of strong and free equals—for the rest of us, Gestalt Tarot is a wonderful gift. Thank you, John McClimans, for creating it.

Appendix I

What Is Gestalt?

The term "Gestalt" was coined by Charles von Ehrenfels in 1890. It is a German term originally meaning form, shape, or configuration. In this century gestaltists have added the meanings "structure, organic whole, and organization."

The Webster's Encyclopedic Unabridged Dictionary of the English Language (Random House Value Publishing, New York, 1996) defines "gestalt" as a "configuration, pattern, or organized field having specific properties that cannot be derived from the summation of its component parts; a unified whole."

The New Columbia Encyclopedia (Columbia University Press, 1975) defines gestalt as a: "School of psychology that interprets phenomena as organized wholes rather than as aggregates of distinct parts and maintains that the whole is more than the sum of its parts . . ." and "studies basic human concerns such as value, order, and meaning." It adds that "In its emphasis on structural wholes, Gestalt psychology has been thought of as analogous to field physics."

Gestalt psychology as a movement began in 1910 in Frankfurt, Germany. Here three psychologists gathered to study the psychology of perception, how the brain sees and interprets visual phenomena. Their names were Max Wertheimer, Wolfgang Kohler, and Kurt Koffka. They were interested in "Apparent movement . . . the perception of motion as a gestalt, a unique property that is not present in the sense elements."

What does that mean? Consider a motion picture, which is composed of thousands of individual pictures strung together on film, shown extremely rapidly, one after another. Intellectually we know that the film cels are individual pictures; but when they are projected we perceive them as continuous movement. You may have experienced this as a child if you made your own cartoon show by drawing stick figures on a pad of paper, then flipping through the pad so the figures seemed to move. Our brains fill in the spaces between the pictures, and make a seamless experience, a whole, a "gestalt" from the bits.

In 1944 Kohler wrote about seeing patterns or wholes, the larger picture: ". . . gestalt findings call for an interpretation 'from above,' because the component parts exhibit characteristics which they owe to their position within the larger entity . . . They have to be interpreted 'from above'; because with this type it is a situation as a whole which determines the behavior of its parts."

The concept of gestalt quickly expanded beyond visual perception to embrace the entire person. In the same year Wertheimer explained that, "There are contexts in which what is happening in the whole cannot be deduced from the characteristics of the separate pieces, but conversely: what happens to a part of the whole is, in clear-cut cases, determined by the laws of the inner structure of the whole."

Koffka defined gestalt as "the attempt to find within the mass of phenomena coherent functional wholes, to treat them as full primary realities and to understand the behavior of these wholes as well as of their parts, from whole rather than from part laws."

In 1936 Kurt Lewin (1890–1947) had defined gestalt as "a system whose parts are dynamically connected in such a way that a change of one part results in a change of all other parts."

So for the first time in recent Western civilization, people were suggesting that human beings should not be viewed as bits and pieces, aggregations of disconnected organs or thoughts or emotions, but as whole beings in whom any part was affected by all the rest. These founders of gestalt went on to contribute a great array of psychological insights: *Prägnanz*, closure, proximity, similarity, symmetry, psychophysical isomorphism, trace theory, insight learning, productive thinking, the isolation effect, and relational theory.

The idea of Prägnanz is sometimes important when you use Gestalt Tarot as a counseling tool. The word is German, and is sometimes translated as "precision" when used in a psychological context. In the 1930s Koffka explained it this way: "According to a very general law of gestalt theory, called the law of Prägnanz, the best possible equilibrium will be achieved . . . psychological organization will always be as 'good' as the prevailing conditions allow." To put it in different terms, even the most neurotic, dysfunctional, messed-up person is doing the best they know how to do under the circumstances. If you understand how the person is put together mentally, and what the circumstances of his life are, then you will understand why they behave as they do.

In 1966, Fritz (Frederick) S. Perls (1893–1970) added a new dimension. In his book *Gestalt Psychotherapy* Perls wrote of, "Viewing the organism-as-a-whole, i.e., the organism-environment unity, the human organism within its environment. The central conception is the theory that the organism is striving for the maintenance of a balance which is continuously disturbed by its needs, and regained through their gratification or elimination." Readers who have studied the Gaia Hypothesis may recognize a startling parallel here: "As above, so below."

In *Gestalt Therapy* (1951) Perls, Ralph E. Hefferline, and Paul Goodman wrote that: "attention, concentration, interest, concern, excitement and grace are representative" of healthy relationships between people and their environments, while "confusion, boredom, compulsions, fixations, anxiety, amnesia, stagnation and self-consciousness" are indicative of disturbed relationships.

Lewin said that "life space [is] the totality of facts or events by which one's behavior is determined at any given moment. Describing behavior in terms of life space is topological psychology, life space being the larger concept engulfing both the person and his environment."

Later Perls, in *Gestalt Therapy Verbatim* (1969), wrote that gestalt therapy is all about "making the person whole and complete again," "developing the human potential," and discovering that "the meaning of life is that it is to be lived."

The famous psychologist Abraham Maslow (1908–1970), known for his "Hierarchy of Human Needs" theory, was profoundly influenced by gestalt psychology. In the 1960s he helped found the Association for Humanistic Psychology, based on four major tenets:

1. Centering of attention on the experiencing person, and thus a focus on experience as the primary phenomenon in the study of man.

2. Emphasis on such distinctively human qualities as choice, creativity, valuation, and self-realization, as opposed to thinking about human beings in mechanistic and reductionistic terms.

3. Allegiance to meaningfulness in the selection of problems for study; opposition to a primary emphasis on objectivity at the expense of significance.

4. An ultimate concern with and valuing of the dignity and worth of man and an interest in the development of the potential inherent in every person." (From a brochure prepared by Charlotte Buhler and James F. T. Bugental).

Most references are from *History and Systems of Psychology*, William S. Sahakian, John Wiley & Sons, New York, 1975.

Appendix II

The Gestalt Reading Step-by-Step

1. Reader and querent agree on the fee or contract.

2. Reader and querent set the appointment.

3. Reader prepares the environment.

4. Reader welcomes the client.

5. Querent and reader develop the question.

6. Querent shuffles the cards while thinking of the question.

7. Querent divides the cards into three stacks, then reassembles them.

8. Querent chooses cards from the top or anywhere in the deck.

9. Querent lays out the cards, face down, wherever each feels right.

10. Querent turns over one card.

11. Reader asks questions, and the card is explored:
    By itself;
    According to its position in the spread; and
    As applied to the querent's question.

12. The process is repeated with each card.

13. When all the cards have been viewed and discussed, look for patterns:

The order in which they were put down;

The order in which they were turned over;

The story in sequence;

Left to right;

Top vs. bottom;

Major vs. minor arcana;

Preponderance of one or two suits; and

Common symbols, colors, figures, etc.

14. Reader summarizes the key points of the reading.

15. Reader offers notes and/or the opportunity to copy the spread.

16. Querent pays the reader if appropriate.

17. Reader thanks the querent and says good-bye.

18. Querent follows through with appropriate action in response to the reading.

Appendix

II

Bibliography

Books About Tarot

Some of the books in this list may be out of print. Contact the publisher first, then we suggest that you seek a copy through Interlibrary Loan or go to one of the bookfinder services on the Internet, such as Powell's in Portland, Oregon (1-800-878-7323 or www.powells.com). An exclamation mark (!) indicates the book is exceptional.

Annotated Reading List

Abraham, Sylvia. *How to Read the Tarot*. St. Paul: Llewellyn Worldwide, 1994.

Akron and Hajo Banzhaf. *The Crowley Tarot; The Handbook to the Cards*. Stamford, Conn.: U.S. Games Systems, 1997. Extensive keys to each card, major and minor, incorporating numerous symbolic and occult systems. Correspondences to the cards include runes, astrology, music, myths, gems, alchemy, and more. A bit of everything; impressive.

Almond, Jocelyn and Keith Seddon. *Understanding Tarot*. N.p.: Thorsons, 1991. Practical tips for beginning card readers; brief, sometimes inaccurate, but not offensive.

Arrien, Angeles. *The Tarot Handbook: Practical Applications of Ancient Visual Symbols*. Chandler, Ariz.: Arcus, 1997. Approaches Tarot through myth and anthropology and relies heavily on numerology and astrology. Good companion book to Crowley and the easiest place to start if you have a Crowley deck but cannot understand Crowley's books. Plenty of useful, thoughtful exercises; clearly written, although her card interpretations become simplistic and formulaic once you catch on.

Ashcroft-Nowicki, Dolores. *Shining Paths: An Experiential Journey through the Tree of Life*. N.p.: Aquarian Press, 1985. Qabalah-based pathworkings, powerful.

Biedermann, Hans. *Dictionary of Symbolism: Cultural Icons and the Meanings Behind Them.* New York: Facts on File, 1992. As it says, from "above/below" to "Zohar, Book of." Has a pictorial index. Very useful reference work.

Buess, Lynn M. *Tarot and Transformation.* New York: Devorss & Co., 1977. Early book on Tarot as a tool for self-exploration and growth: some pathworking, some meditation techniques, as well as interpretations of the cards.

Butler, Bill. *Dictionary of the Tarot.* Shocken Books, 1975. Compares symbols and images of various traditional decks (*Rider-Waite-Smith, Marseilles, Aquarian, Crowley*) and offers interpretations from renowned Tarot experts and occultists.

Case, Paul Foster. *The Tarot: A Key to the Wisdom of the Ages.* McCoy, Richmond, Vir., 1947. B.O.T.A., 1995. Case, a major figure in the Builders of the Adytum, presents the deck's major arcana in some detail. The BOTA system is based in the magickal traditions of the Masons, Rosicrucians, and the Qabalah. Other books by Case are recommended to those interested in any of these systems.

Cavendish, Richard. *The Tarot.* London: Michael Joseph, 1975. A large, heavily illustrated encyclopedia of Tarot history and lore. Very nice.

Cirlot, J. E. *A Dictionary of Symbols.* N.p.: Dorset Press, 1991. Alphabetically-arranged comparative study of symbols in an effort to understand and define their essential meaning. Prefatory essays on symbolism. (Spanish version still in print.)

Connolly, Eileen. *Tarot: A New Handbook for the Apprentice.* North Hollywood, Calif.: Newcastle, 1979, 1990. Connolly joins Tarot with astrology, numerology and Qabalah and provides lots of exercises, in workbook fashion. In two volumes (continues with Journeyman and Master). Uses the Connolly deck.

Crowley, Aleister (The Master Therion). *The Book of Thoth.* York Beach, Maine: Samuel Weiser, 1981. Crowley's own tome on his "Egyptian Tarot" deck based on the Golden Dawn system of magick. Cryptic for the beginning user; try Arrien or Akron and Banzhaf first.

Douglas, Alfred. *The Tarot: The Origins, Meaning and Uses of the Cards.* New York: Viking Penguin, 1992. Good general book touching on all aspects of the Tarot. Has a decent bibliography.

Dummett, Michael. *The Visconti-Sforza Tarot Cards.* Scranton, Penn.: George Braziller, 1986. Color reproductions of many of the seventy-four surviving cards of the famous deck first produced in the fifteenth century. Offers a little history and commentary, but this is not a book on divination. Nice, especially if you do not want to buy this deck but want to see the images.

! Fairfield, Gail. *Everyday Tarot* (formerly *Choice Centered Tarot*). New York: Samuel Weiser, 1997. Cogent and clearly written, and much of it can be applied to the Gestalt Tarot method.

Guiley, Rosemary Ellen. *The Mystical Tarot.* New York: Signet Books, 1991. Better than the average book on Tarot; intelligent, well written, good introduction.

Jayanti, Amber. *Living the Tarot*. St. Paul: Llewellyn Worldwide, 1999. Uses the Builders of the Adytum deck to map a system of personal growth and discovery; pathworking with each major arcanum. Illustrations of cards are uncolored and a coloring key is given at the back, along with a brief list of correspondences. The author's belief is that the plethora of artistic decks now available are not the true Tarot of the Western mystery traditions.

Jung, Carl Gustav. *Alchemical Studies*. Princeton: Bollingen, 1967. Five essays of incredible range and depth explore the psychological and religious implications of personal development, spirit, and the archetypes.

———. *Man and His Symbols*. New York: Doubleday, 1964. A wide-ranging exploration of the human psyche and the many ways it is expressed in art around the world and through time.

! Kaplan, Stuart R. *The Encyclopedia of Tarot*, Vols. I, II, III. Stamford, Conn.: U.S. Games Systems, 1978, 1985, 1990. (ncludes superb annotated bibliography. Extensive reference work on the Tarot, covering history and documenting many decks in and out of print.

Kopp, Sheldon. *The Hanged Man: Psychotherapy and the Forces of Darkness*. Palo Alto, Calif.: Science and Behavior Books, 1974. Not the usual thing; a very personal book about the author's psychotherapy career and his impending death, against the backdrop of some Major Arcana Tarot images.

Nichols, Sallie. *Jung and Tarot, An Archetypal Journey*. York Beach, Maine: Samuel Weiser, 1980. Interpretations of the Tarot in Jungian terms, especially relying on universal symbols in art to underscore and amplify the Major Arcana.

Ouspensky, P. D. *The Symbolism of the Tarot: Philosophy of Occultism in Pictures and Numbers*. Kila, Mont.: Kessinger Pub. Co., 1998. Esoteric visions of Ouspensky and their relation to traditional Tarot symbols. Originally published in Russia in 1913.

Papus. *The Tarot of the Bohemians: The Absolute Key to Occult Science*. North Hollywood, Calif.: Wilshire Book Co., 1982. Earlier centuries brought us the mystical Tarot through the occult revival periods of the eighteenth century up to the twentieth. Papus' book is one of these early ones, suitably esoteric and intentionally obscure. Interesting from an historical perspective.

Riley, Jana. *The Tarot Book*. York Beach, Maine: Samuel Weiser, 1992. Approaches reading the cards from Jungian and psychological perspectives. Explores archetypes and personality types; especially sensible techniques for reading court cards. Interesting.

———. *Tarot Dictionary and Compendium*. York Beach, Maine: Samuel Weiser, 1995. What Butler (above) did for the traditional decks, Riley continues with more contemporary ones, giving interpretations from authors like Arrien, Greer, Fairfield, Crowley, Noble, and Pollack, among others.

Shavick, Nancy. *Traveling the Royal Road: Mastering the Tarot*. East Rutherford, N.J.: Berkley Books, 1992. All of Shavick's books are hand-scribed and worth looking into; this book uses a karmic approach and emphasizes personal growth and understanding of oneself on a cosmic level.

Stuart, Micheline. *The Tarot: Path to Self Development*. Boston: Shambhala, 1996. This slim book describes the journey of the Fool as applied to Gurdjieff's teachings on self-development. Illustrated with the *Marseilles* deck.

Waite, Arthur Edward. *The Pictorial Key to the Tarot*. New York: Carol Publishing Group, 1979. The classic by the most influential modern Tarot designer. Like Papus' book, this one is sometimes intentionally poetic and obscure to noninitiates. Based on his own *Rider-Waite-Smith* deck.

Walker, Barbara. *The Secrets of the Tarot: Origins, History and Symbolism*. Stamford, Conn.: U.S. Games Systems, 1997. Walker examines the symbols and stories of the Tarot from a global, mythic standpoint with a bent toward feminist interpretation. Interesting multicultural imagery and viewpoints. Based on her own deck.

Wang, Robert. *The Qabalistic Tarot: A Textbook of Mystical Philosophy*. York Beach, Maine: Samuel Weiser, 1987. Excellent book by a respected Tarot author and deck designer (*Golden Dawn Tarot* with Israel Regardie). Valuable.

Other Books Worth Consideration

Ando, Arnell. *Transformational Tarot*. Montara, Calif.: Ink Well Publishing, 1995.

Ashcroft-Nowicki, Dolores. *Highways of the Mind: The Art and History of Pathworking*. N.p.: Aquarian Press, 1987.

———. *Inner landscapes: A Journey into Awareness by Pathworking*. N.p.:Aquarian Press, 1989. Uses *Servants of the Light Tarot*.

Banzhaf, Hajo. *Tarot and the Journey of the Hero*. York Beach, Maine: Samuel Weiser, 2000.

Bennett, Sidney. *Tarot for the Millions*. Los Angeles: Sherbourne, 1967.

Bias, Clifford, ed. *Qabalah, Tarot & the Western Mystery Tradition: The 22 Connecting Paths of the Tree of Life*. York Beach, Maine: Samuel Weiser, 1997.

Cicero, Chic and Sandra Tabatha Cicero. *The Golden Dawn Magical Tarot*. St. Paul: Llewellyn Worldwide, 2000. Uses the deck of the same name.

Denning, Melita, and Osborne Phillips. *The Llewellyn Practical Guide to the Magick of the Tarot: How to Read, and Shape, Your Future*. St. Paul: Llewellyn Worldwide, 1983.

Doane, Doris Chase, and King Keyes. *How to Read Tarot Cards*. New York: Funk & Wagnalls, 1967. Uses the *Egyptian Tarot* deck.

Doane, Doris Chase. *Secret Symbolism of the Tarot*. Tempe, Ariz.: American Federation of Astrologers, 1993.

Encausse, Gerard. *Tarot of the Bohemians: The Most Ancient Book in the World for the Use of Initiates*. Kila, Mont.: Kessinger Pub. Co., 1998, reprint of 1914.

Galenorn, Yasmine. *Tarot Journeys; Adventures in Self-Transformation*. St. Paul: Llewellyn Worldwide, 1999.

Gerulskis-Estes, Susan. *The Book of Tarot*. Keene Valley, N.Y.: Morgan & Morgan, 1981. Uses the *Morgan-Greer* deck.

Giles, Cynthia. *The Tarot: History, Mystery, and Lore*. New York: Simon & Schuster, 1994

Gordon, Richard, and Dixie Taylor. *Intuitive Tarot: A Metaphysical Approach to Reading the Tarot Cards*. Nevada City, Calif.: Blue Dolphin Publishing, 1994

Graves, F. D. *The Windows of Tarot*. Keene Valley, N.Y.: Morgan & Morgan,1973.

Gray, Eden. *Mastering the Tarot*. East Rutherford, N.J.: New American Library, 1995. Uses the *Rider-Waite-Smith* deck.

———. *The Tarot Revealed*. East Rutherford, N.J.: New American Library, 1995. Uses the *Rider-Waite-Smith* deck.

Greer, Mary. *Tarot Constellations: Patterns of Personal Destiny*. Stamford, Conn.: U.S. Games Systems, 1997.

———. *Tarot for Your Self: A Workbook for Personal Transformation*. Stamford, Conn.: U.S. Games Systems, 1997.

———. *Tarot Mirrors: Reflections of Personal Meaning*. Stamford, Conn.: U.S. Games Systems, 1997.

Gwain, Rose. *Discovering Yourself Through the Tarot: A Jungian Guide to Archetypes and Personality*. Rochester, Ver.: Inner Traditions International, Ltd., 1993.

Hoeller, Stephan A. *The Royal Road: A Manual of Kabalistic Meditations on the Tarot*. Wheaton, Ill.: Theosophical Publishing, 1990. Uses the *Rider-Waite-Smith* deck.

Huson, Paul. *The Devil's Picturebook*. London: Abacus, 1971.

Junjulas, Craig. *Psychic Tarot*. Stamford, Conn.: U.S. Games Systems, 1992. Uses the *Aquarian* deck.

Kaplan, Stuart R. *Tarot Cards for Fun and Fortune Telling*. Stamford, Conn.: U.S. Games Systems, 1970. Book accompanies the *Swiss IJJ* deck (Müller & Cie, Switzerland).

Kliegman, Isabel. *Tarot & the Tree of Life: Finding Everyday Wisdom in the Minor Arcana*. Wheaton, Ill.: Theosophical Publishing House, 1997.

Knight, Gareth. *Tarot and Magic: Images for Rituals and Pathworking*. Rochester, Ver.: Destiny, 1986, 1991. Uses the *Marseilles* deck.

———. *Magical World of the Tarot*. York Beach, Maine: Samuel Weiser, 1996.

Lyle, Jane. *The Key to the Tarot*. San Francisco: HarperSanFrancisco, 1993.

McLaine, Patricia. *The Wheel of Destiny*. Camden, Maine: Akasha Publishing, 1999.

Moore, Daphna. *The Rabbi's Tarot*. Llewellyn Worldwide, St. Paul, 1999. Qabalistic pathworkings for the major arcana.

Pollack, Rachel. *Seventy-Eight Degrees of Wisdom*. London: Aquarian Press, 1988.

Renée, Janina. *Tarot Spells*. St. Paul: Llewellyn Worldwide,1996.

Sadhu, Mouni. *The Tarot*. Los Angeles, Borden Pub. Co., 1940. Basically the *Rider-Waite-Smith* deck.

Sharman-Burke, Juliet. *The Complete Book of Tarot.* New York: St. Martin's Press, 1996. Uses the *Rider-Waite-Smith* deck.

Shavick, Nancy. *Nancy Shavick's Tarot Universe.* Santa Monica: Santa Monica Press, 1999.

———. *The Tarot: A Guide to Reading Your Own Cards.* East Rutherford, N.J.: Berkley Books, 1988.

———. *The Tarot Reader.* E. Rutherford, N.J.: Berkley Books, 1991.

Walker, Ann. *The Living Tarot.* N.p.: Holmes Publishing Group, 1994.

Zain, C. C. *The Sacred Tarot: The Ancient Art of Card Reading & the Underlying Spiritual Science.* Los Angeles: The Church of Light, 1994. Uses the *Egyptian Tarot.*

Periodical

Greer, Mary Katherine. "The Three-Card Spread." *Tarot Network News,* vol.1 #2: 5, 1983.

Audio Cassettes

Gordon, Richard. *How to Read the Tarot Cards.* Nevada City, Calif.: Blue Dolphin, 1994.

Hamaker-Sondag, Karen. *Tarot as a Way of Life: A Jungian Approach to the Tarot.* York Beach, Maine: Samuel Weiser, 1997.

Candlemas: Feast of Flames

Amber K and Azrael Arynn K

*The only book devoted to Brigid's Festival of Returning Light—
an ancient holiday filled with hope*

Beyond the darkness of winter, there is an oasis of light and warmth on the journey from solstice to spring. Known as Candlemas, Imbolc, Brigantia, or Lupercus, it is a celebration held in early February to welcome the returning light. Celtic Goddess Brigid presides, and it's customary to light candles to observe the sun's rebirth.

Candlemas is filled with customs and traditions from a variety of cultures—Irish, British, Scots, Welsh, Norwegian, Greek, Roman, and Chinese. There are tales from medieval Ireland, delicious recipes, crafts, decorations, detailed rituals, and even magickal spells with candles you make yourself. Post-holiday blues, begone!

- Part of Llewellyn's successful series on each of the Pagan sabbats, or holidays
- Both authors are well-known throughout the Pagan community
- For anyone who celebrates the turning of the seasons and the ancient holy days
- Relevant to any culturally based path

0-7387-0079-7, 360 pp., 7½ x 9⅛   **$14.95**